...Growing up knowing that I was different from everyone else around me was frightening and lowered my opinion of myself even further than what most teenagers experience. What I needed, and didn't have, was somebody, anybody, to tell me that I wasn't alone...Teachers, parents and peers so strongly affect our sense of who we are. They can plant the seeds for healthier and happier young adults who fear what it means to have the feelings they do...TWENTY-FIRST CENTURY CHALLENGE offers insight into the minds and hearts of our students and educators so that the pain I experienced could be prevented...

- **Anita Pace, Editor: WRITE FROM THE HEART; LESBIANS HEALING FROM HEARTACHE and Author: IF YOU WANT TO SOAR, YOU'VE GOT TO FLY. Publisher of Baby Steps Press, Or.**

...Finally, here is a book that needed to be written. Lesbians and Gays in Education comes out of the closet. For too long, lesbians and gays in the schools have been a "dirty little secret".
  Ms. McConnell-Celi, a long time human rights proponent and activist within the lesbian and gay community, should be congratulated for writing about the obvious.

- **Michael Singervalt, School Psychologist and Founder of Gay and Lesbian Youth, NJ.**

...This fascinating anthology provides a glimpse into the world of lesbians and gays in the classroom. It demonstrates that greater inclusion and diversity will not only enhance the curriculum, but hopes to raise EVERY STUDENT'S potentiality and sense of self esteem.
  More than any profession, educators are in a position to create understanding and social harmony. TWENTY-FIRST CENTURY CHALLENGE: LESBIANS AND GAYS IN EDUCATION - BRIDGING THE GAP offers that opportunity...Easily, teachers can include materials from this book in their lessons. It reflects a variety of experiences - humorous and serious, as well as practical classroom suggestions to set the pace for change.

- **Dr. Virginia Uribe, Educator, Founder of Project 10 in California, Pioneer in Lesbian and Gay High School Counseling affecting programs nationwide.**

TWENTY-FIRST CENTURY CHALLENGE

LESBIANS AND GAYS IN EDUCATION

Bridging the Gap

Edited by Sue McConnell-Celi

New Jersey

Sue McConnell-Celi received her B.S. in Education from Seton
Hall University and M.A. in Reading Specialization from Kean College.
A language arts teacher for 22 years, she had taught grades 7 through
college. This fifty-year old grandmother of five has been an active
human rights proponent since the '60's. As a former journalist/columnist,
she covered human interest and political stories for more than a decade,
while frequently holding executive board memberships in League of
Women Voters and the National Exchange Club. As a teacher,
she advised school newspapers and the yearbook; past editor of both
(though not simultaneously) local AFT and NEA publications.
A member of the church choir and local Opera Repertoire Company
in the '80's, other achievements include lesbian and gay radio shows
(producer and co-host) for both New Jersey (On the Line) and New York/
Connecticut based Pacifica Radio, and co-facilitator for workshops in
lesbigay education or lesbian/feminist herstory for Sisterspace, Pennsylvania;
New Jersey Education Association, Atlantic City Teacher's Convention;
Bloomfield College, Gay Activist Alliance of Morris County, and local
school districts. A published poet in LESBIAN LIVES, COMMON LIVES,
a literary magazine, WRITE FROM THE HEART (Baby Steps Press)
and NETWORK Magazine, her works have also appeared in SAPPHO'S ISLE
and LAVENDER EXPRESS. Community activism reaches
back nearly 25 years where she held membership in the oldest
Lesbian Organization in America, the Daughters of Bilitis (NY chpt).
At that time, this mother of four initiated a Lesbian Mother's Union
(in the early days of N.O.W.), and launched the first Gay Activist Alliance
(Essex County) whose members went on to help co-found other GAA groups.
The 1991 recipient of the New Jersey Lesbian and Gay Achievement
Awards. Had the distinguished honor of being the first Lesbian Human
Relations Commissioner in her state, 1990 - 1992, along with dozens of
other community, religious, legal and educational leaders, to help
forge a new future of equality for ALL people.

LAVENDER CRYSTAL PRESS
P.O. Box 8932, Red Bank, NJ 07701

Front cover illustration, SCHOOL OPEN HOUSE, a Dawn Manna Production creation.
Back cover poster, THE WINGSPAN MINISTRY, courtesy of Leo Treadway.

Copyright © 1993 by Sue McConnell-Celi

Library of Congress Catalog Card Number: 93-78393

All rights reserved, including the right to reproduce this book or portions thereof in any form
whatsoever. For information contact Lavender Crystal Press, P.O. Box 8932, Red Bank, N.J. 07701

ISBN: 0-9636909-0-6

Printed in the U.S.A.

Acknowledgements

I would like to thank the following authors, publishers, and organizations for written permission to reprint their works:

Dr. Virginia Uribe for permission to reprint materials from PROJECT 10. Cecilia Tan of Beacon Press for permission to reprint two and a half pages from ANOTHER MOTHER TONGUE: GAY WORDS, GAY WORLDS, 1984 by Judy Grahn. Lynn Lavner, composer/singer of "Anne Frank", 1988 on the Bent Album for permission to reprint the song and her story. Cooper Thompson of the Campaign To End Homophobia, Cambridge, Mass., for permission to reprint portions of I THINK I MIGHT BE A LESBIAN and I THINK I MIGHT BE GAY..NOW WHAT DO I DO? Richard Jennings, Executive Director of GLAAD, LA for permission to reprint sections of HOMOPHOBIA: Discrimination Based on Sexual Orientation, a curriculum packet. Chris Kaplan, publisher of THE NETWORK, N.J.'s LESBIAN AND GAY MAGAZINE, and Jeffrey Krell for permission to use one JAYSON cartoon. Leo Treadway for permission to print poster WHAT DO I DO? from the Wingspan Ministry of St. Paul-Reformation Lutheran Church, Saint Paul, Minn. GAY SCOTLAND MAGAZINE, Edinburgh, England, for permission to reprint COMING OUT- AS A TEACHER by Henry D. Robertson. Ben Marshall and Middlesex County College for permission to use the Lesbian and Gay Literature Course Reading List. Mr. Tracy Phariss of The Teachers' Group of Colorado for permission to print A BIBLIOGRAPHY; GAY AND LESBIAN ISSUES IN EDUCATION. Craig Rodwell, proprietor of the Oscar Wilde Memorial Bookstore, New York City for granting the right to print the labrys/pink triangle logo and explanation. Carole Johnson for permission to reprint sections from STICKS, STONES AND STEREOTYPES, Equity Institute Inc, Amherst, Mass. Barry Murray, editor of THE CAPITAL SPOTLIGHT for permission to reprint portions of article by Leonard Green (author has also granted permission). Rosalie McGovern, Adm., Intellectual Property Rights Board of the US Postal Service for expressed permission to reproduce copyrighted US postage stamps. Paul Hennefeld for permission to reproduce The Lesbians and Gays On Stamps Collection. Demian, editor of PARTNERS TASK FORCE, Seattle Washington, for their paragraph on mothers. Charles Haver, creator of "Bittersweet" cartoons for permission to use seven comic strips. Dawn Manna for permission to use her drawings and cartoons. Pink Panthers for permission to use their suggestions. Pop Against Homophobia, England and USA for their permission to use a variety of their poster reproductions. Pat Freeman, editor of LAVENDER EXPRESS, NJ for permission to use paragraph, "Lifeshare". Susan Cavin, author of LESBIAN ORIGINS and publisher ISM for permission to repreduce "Hystery Coin Toss" chart and page excerpts. Jessea Greenman for her "opinion piece". THE CORMORANT, Canada, editor William Poulty for permission to reprint THE MANLY KISS. Dell Richards for use of taped radio message. Paul Hanson for granting permission to reproduce the stamp collection. Tam Garson for her photos, WE REFUSE TO DISAPPEAR and MAN WITH COMPUTER. Dr. Sylvia K. Baer, editor of TRANSFORMATIONS, the New Jersey Project based at William Paterson College with imput from other colleges, for permission to reprint portions of John Kellermeier's article from Volume 3, Number 2. John Kellermeier for his consent as well as his creation of new word problems in diversity. Jean Sidebottom, publisher of SAPPHO'S ISLE for Book Review.

special thanks to -
All the contributors of **TWENTY-FIRST CENTURY CHALLENGE:**
Lesbians and Gays in Education - Bridging the Gap *for their faith & insight.*

My four children for their patience, adaptability and courage; may the world be a safer place for their children.

The school staff, administration and parents for remaining steadfast and supportive as I was named NJ's first Lesbian Human Relations Commissioner.

The progressive Lesbian and Gay Educators of New Jersey.

The Lesbians of the Light in sharing their journey toward wholeness.

The Lincroft Lesbian Rap Group, Slightly Older Lesbians (SOL), and the Hoboken Lesbians and Gays in Literature and the Arts discussion group, providing intellectual and emotional sustenance these years.

The N.J. Lesbian and Gay Coalition who opened the door to my first radio opportunities and the dynamic Gay and Lesbian Independent Broadcasters, NY.

The myriad radio guests; they gave of their time and energy to create change in the world, especially those courageous People with AIDS and breast or cervical cancer. We hope that a cure is found soon.

My therapist, a gentlewoman, who skillfully led me to make appropriate changes in my life.

My sisters and brother, for their unswerving belief in my judgement.
My Dad, who died twenty years ago, but whose vivacious personality lives on.
My Mom - she taught me life-long lessons in fairness, determination.

vi

Preface

Three years ago, I began a national search for writings and drawings that express the lesbian/gay experience in the field of education. Within the first year, I had over 50 items - personal narratives, essays, poems, brief comments, cartoons and one full length novel - exemplifying that silence is not golden for the lesbian or gay teacher or student. Almost everybody was ready to cooperate in this project. In addition, due to the wonderful publications put out by the community, various discussion groups, lesbian/gay bookstores, and the LESBIAN HERSTORY ARCHIVES, I was able to glean additional information in what I term, LESBIGAY LITERACY. However, following an operation and partial disability in 1991, the stories were put on hold - until now.

Faced with the problem of organizing the enormous variety of materials, I sent the manuscripts off to three publishing houses. Valuable suggestions were made by each, but the work was too long and unwieldy to be taken seriously. I then began to view it with a much needed critical eye - less is more, and decide upon your audience - advice I routinely gave my writing classes did not come easily to me. In the meanwhile, several of the writers had their works published elsewhere. With the enormous need for improved AIDS instruction, the high suicide and drop-out rates among lesbian and gay teens, and the hoopla over the Rainbow Curriculum, the spotlight had shifted to education. Finally, people were starting to realize that no one wins when a life is lost.

This anthology is comprised of three major sections. You will notice the first section reveals the coming out process reflected in poems and personal narratives from an herstorical/historical perspective - the DISCOVERY that individuals initially make about themselves or others within a certain time frame. Teachers from diverse backgrounds and levels of instruction ranging from grade 4 through college are beginning to close the book on stereotype and stigma. UNDERSTANDING LESBIAN AND GAY YOUTH, part two, speaks for itself, as do these observant contributors. From the corridor to the classroom, these young people have thrived, as well as survived to find themselves standing on the threshold of a harmonious, new world. To help them cross that threshold, parents and teachers must create fair curricula, implemented by accurate textbooks. Everyone can profit from inclusion. Dr. Virginia Uribe, nationally renown pioneer in lesbigay school counseling programs, indicates that hetereosexual children are also best served when terms like "dyke" and "fag" no longer have a stranglehold over them, steering them into gender roles that delimit or they are not comfortable with. And given the loss of self-esteem that girls ages 9 and up experience, studies of lesbians who transcended these female societal restrictions would certainly benefit our students. Part three, the VISION, shares a bit of our culture, and demonstrates a few basic teaching strategies, in hopes that new ideas will be spawned. The possibilities are as limitless as the pebbles on the beach. Or the number of school districts in the nation.

Who should read TWENTY-FIRST CENTURY CHALLENGE? Of course, lesbians, gay men and bisexuals - we are all from educational institutions. Parents should read it - too long have they borne the brunt of social ostracism, passing it onto their lesbian or gay child. Libraries could stock the anthology for the general reading public. Bookstores at shopping malls can carry it.

And mainly teachers themselves - whether secondary school or college level - might utilize the information in this book for practical classroom use. Teachers are the vital key. More than any other occupation, they alone possess the sensibilities and expertise to take up the challenge, bringing us closer to the promise of change that we envision for the twenty-first century.

- Sue McConnell-Celi
May, 1993

CONTENTS

Preface

ILLUSTRATIONS, POSTERS, PHOTOS AND CARTOONS

For all those
who care enough
about humankind
to open this book

PART I

DISCOVERY

Coming Out
To
Students
And
Staff

Early Memories
poem by Lee Headman

When and where did it all begin, the attraction of the same sex?
With my best friend Evelyn, my pal, my buddy?
We galloped through neighborhood yards on imaginary horses...
We called ourselves Dusty and Rusty and kept
 Our wonder horses in a hidden cave unknown to all but us
In her back yard...
We played pretend under the bed of her small room...
We kissed not knowing how,
We touched not knowing why,
And went out to ride our horses once again...
I was ten.

The games played with Betty...
I was always Tarzan,
She was always Jane,
I was always Roy Rogers,
She was always Dale Evans.
I saved her time and time again from many jungle perils
We wrestled in the back seat of her father's Ford,
Overacting the scenes from last Saturday's matinee at the Regent
I was kissing just like they did in the movies,
And touching, that somehow caused unexplained feelings,
I may have played doctor a few times,
Always enjoyed the adventurous roles and much more...
I was twelve.

I was too much involved with sports in my early teen years
To give much thought to girls sexually...
The friends I did have were very straight and I went along
     with them to slumber parties, the Crystal Palace for ice
     cream and just listened as they talked about boys...
Boys were to play softball and basketball with; admiration
     for them was how they handled a bat or a basketball,
I was never attracted to boys sexually..
I had great friends at this time, Bessie, Barbara, and Anne,
We were close and I think of them today with tenderness...
I was sixteen.

High school was a horror!
I still maintained my female friends,
But gradually lost them to dates and proms...
I missed them and then I met Barbara
Beautiful blonde and blue-eyed Barbara
Cheerleader, chosen most popular girl
In the high school yearbook...
I managed to be chosen one of the class clowns
I did have a great sense of humor...
An evening at Barbara's house...
Her parents out for the evening...
We were lying across her bed
Watching the horse show on television...
(Honest!)
"How do you kiss?" she asked...
"With my mouth," I replied (living up to my title)
She moved in close to me, put her arms around me,

4

And pressed her mouth to mine...
Now this was not lips pressed tight together,
But lips apart soft and moist...
Something moved somewhere deep inside me,
And I naturally put my arms around her,
Our bodies touching...
We necked (that's what it was called in the fifties)
For a long time...
I was breathless and confused...
Her parents came home and it was time for me to leave,
I walked home elated and frightened out of my wits,
I couldn't understand my feelings...
Was I a lezzie?
Was I a queer?
I never "made out" with Barbara again...
We were close friends, but never intimate...
I was seventeen.

I became involved with the PAL and basketball was my life...
Then into my life came Dot
What a great basketball player she was!
She pegged me immediately and loved to tease me,
Laughing at my innocence and confusion...
I will always be grateful to Dot, for she brought me out...
I was never involved with her sexually,
But she did talk me into going to New York with her,
On a Friday night to the Club Bagatelle in Greenwich Village...
I was terrified as we walked into the dimly lit bar...
All I had to go on was what I read or heard

About Greenwich Village and this was certainly
Not positive...
I entered the bar to discover it filled with women,
My fright gave way to a feeling of - this is where I belong...
I made the Bagatelle my home every weekend for many years,
Here I met the most wonderful women...
Jean, Tanya, Bobbie, Diane, Rose, Pat...
Where are they all today?
Did I ever tell you that I love you?...
I was eighteen.

This "coming out" time was during the fabulous fifties...
The days of queer bashings...
The days of police raids...
The days of butches and femmes...
The days of sexual freedom for me,
The unexperienced kid from a small town who believed she was
The only "queer" in the world...
Dancing all night long on weekends,
Going for breakfast in the early moring hours with friends...
Sunday brunches at the Bagatelle...
Hot, sunny afternoons at Riis Park's "gay beach"...
House parties and women, women, women!
I certainly had my share of sexual experiences and
Romantically wined and dined many wonderful women...
I brought flowers to them...
I sang to them...
I danced with them...
I loved them...

6

The sweet smell of perfume in their hair...
Their laughter, the sharing of new experiences...
The discovery of new places and things...
"See the Pyramids Along the Nile"...
"I Only Have Eyes For You"...
The Cha Cha...
The Fish...
The Lindy...
Broken Hearts...
New romances...
Learning and growing...
There were no support groups...
No gay rights...
No one to fight for us (we protected each other)...
All was not roses...I lost friends to drugs...
Lost them to mental institutions, (put there by parents and
Psychiatrists who viewed homosexuality as a mental illness)...
Lost them to suicide (unable to cope with their sexuality
   in a hostile world)...
Lost them to the streets and the gangs who came into the Village
Specifically to "beat on queers"...
Some found it easier to go back to the "straight" world...
But somehow, there were many of us who survived
And continued to do it our way...
I was nineteen...
I was twenty...
I was twenty-two...
These are just some of my Early Memories.

Lee Headman ❖ *Lee is a published poet and the co-founder of LAMBDA ALLIANCE, a New Jersey based lesbian and gay organization, 1980-85. A former employee of a local Women's Crisis Center, she has an extensive background of helping people help themselves. Currently the originator and coordinator of an innovative hospital ambulance service, she has special concerns with the environment, the rainforest and animal life, participating every year in SAVE THE WHALE. Lee formerly owned an antique shop in Jersey.*

POP AGAINST HOMOPHOBIA is a youth culture advertising campaign, an exciting brand new concept. PAH advertising campaigns are launched throughout the world and feature affectionate same-sex couples to create positive, contemporary images.

LIKE A SUMMER BREEZE...

poem by Sue McConnell-Cell

Like a summer breeze, she stirs the air with her presence,
enchancing the moment. I breathe in her stillness,
a gift; she expects nothing in return but for me to be there too.
Whether seated on the beige, plush padding of her living room couch
eyeballing bigger-than-life characters on an outsized screen,
or the hard wooden plank of the train seat that we rushed to get
in time after school, craning our necks to glimpse
flickering window-framed scenes that zoom by,
telling stories with each shot
-about the latest international video at
Lesbian Night at the Movies
or the Gay Liberation March of an earlier day,
I inhale her presence.
On the familiar streets of New York, we stride-walk two abreast,
linked arm in arm -
no pressure, no demand -
debris swirls around us in the frantic wind.
It is dusk.
Surrounded by moonbeam yellow, red, and pea-green neon
tubes that shape the night,
We arrive at our destination.

Sue McConnell-Celi and family at the Lesbian and Gay Pride March, early '70's.

SPECTACLES OR NOT
A MESSAGE TO A FEW   by David P. Altier

You wrap arms round your gal by the cinema lite.
We attend on our best behavior.
I look at him, he, me, enough said, we'll go home tonite.

You pronounce your everlasting love to friends, family,
colleagues in public ceremony, approved by church and state,
sealed by rings proclaiming once and for all that you're for
her and she's for you - they witness your first kiss and
know what you're doing that nite.
You tell us to keep our affairs private.

I tell my older friend, the sexual child, the taunted
artist, to conceal his play from the straightwise world. I
say, "You're making a spectacle of yourself." He says, "If
I could cry, I would."

I combat your shame; struggle for pride; yet, you pound me
and hound me with tormenting laughter, shrill as a sea
gull's cry, with judgements such as, "You pervert, you
sinner, repent lest we banish you for eternal punishment,
keep your matters private lest you corrupt the little ones."

I read that phobic seamen, fearful of their own secret
desires, bludgeon a brother mute to death.
You say, "Keep the matter private."

How can you hold hands in the park and condemn me for doing the same?
You say, "keep the matter private,"
but you mean, "don't muddle my world, I'd rather sleep."

That's OK. You're entitled to your opinion, however misguided. You may have been twisted, sheltered, over-disciplined, or berated. You've got a story too. I shan't deny you, yours. And I throw you a loving kiss. You can duck, turn the other cheek, or do whatever else you may fancy.

ABOUT THE POET

David P. Altier ❖ *Certified in N.J. as Teacher of the Handicapped, has taught in public and private settings for mainstreamed and disabled populations. He is dedicated to the principles of democracy and reward in the classroom and has written essays describing such programs and expects one to be published in 1993. He is a voting delegate to the N.J. Lesbian and Gay Coalition and a member of the Legislative Committee.*

EASY RIDE: EPISODE IN A BRITISH ACADEMIC CAREER

by Gregory Woods

1966-70

I was sent to a minor Catholic public school because my father, uncle and elder brother had all been there before me. Notorious as "hotbeds" of homosexuality, the English public schools had prepared generations of adolescents for the rigours of imperial life by policing them with Greek and Latin, rugby football, beatings, and cold baths.

We boys knew the rumours about single-sex boarding schools, and did our best to live up to them. All our gossip was about each other's relationships. We knew who fancied whom; notes were passed, encounters arranged; even the idea of love was not beyond our narrow comprehension. After all, if homosexuality was a phase most boys passed through at puberty, we might as well pass through it with joy. It was assumed we could discreetly do more or less as we liked for the time being, so long as we had stopped being "queer" when we left. It was

12

those of us who believed we would not become heterosexual, who had the least relaxed time of it. What with all the fear and guilt, our love life was rarely hot.

We watched the distant outside world with interest. The passing of the 1967 Sexual Offences Act partially legalized sex between (members of the same sex) over 21. We read the small-ads in OZ and INTERNATIONAL TIMES. Most of us learned the new use of the word "gay."

In my final year, while looking through the files of the school's Law Society, I found a letter from the Homosexual Law Reform Society. It was a brief expression of regret that the school group had been forced to withdraw its invitation to a speaker. No other outside speaker - humanist or communist or whatever - had ever been vetoed.

1970

It occurred to me that, without ignoring or going against what I had been taught, my best strategy for exam-passing was to concentrate on subjects that interested me. So for my History Of Art A-Level, I wrote a dissertation on Donatello and an essay on R.B. Kitaj and David Hockney. In both, I tackled the question of sexuality, if not head-on, at least in the oblique manner that I judged to be expedient.

When it came to English, I found myself writing an essay on Hamlet's relationship with Horatio. Apparently, I had already learned (but not actually been taught) the limits of academic openness: for although my essay proposed a homosexual relationship, my concluding paragraph dismissed the very idea.

The strategy worked. My enthusiasm was rewarded with higher grades than any of my teachers had predicted.

Before leaving school I had read what now seems to me quite an impressive array of gay literature, from Peter Whigham's translations of Catullus to Mann's DEATH IN VENICE, Plato's SYNPOSIUM to Baldwin's GIOVANNI'S ROOM and ANOTHER COUNTRY. I had found Thom Gunn's THE SENSE OF MOVEMENT in the school library, and drawn up my own conclusions about its hidden meanings. Already a compulsive browser in second-hand bookshops, I had mustered a small collection of contemporary gay fiction, both English and American...It laid the foundation for my subsequent scholarship.

What strikes me as most interesting from my present perspective is that, although I was in the middle of one of the most expensive and elitist educations offered anywhere in the world, as a gay man, I was an autodidact. All of my gay cultural knowledge was self-taught.

1971

I went to one of Britain's new, purpose-built universities, which prided themselves on their modernity and progressiveness.

In my first week as an undergraduate, during a seminar on W.H. Auden's poem, "Lay Your Sleeping Head, My Love," we spoke of the poem's addressee as "she" throughout the first hour of our discussion. Finally, our tutor told us Auden was homosexual. Did this information, he asked, change the meaning of the poem?

True to the liberalism expected of our generation, we

14

decided at once that there was no significant, qualitative difference between homosexual and heterosexual love, and none, therefore, between the love the poems might produce. We handled the knowledge that Auden was gay, in other words, by denying that it mattered he was gay.

I doubted our argument, and went back to my room feeling that the issue had not been faced. But I was not equipped, with either confidence or evidence, to have argued the contrary view.

1972

A seminar on Allen Ginsberg's "America," led by a young, male lecturer with long hair and fashionable earrings. When asked if the poet was a homosexual, he replied, "Oh yes, queer as a coot!" Students giggled. After twenty years I can still hear the lecturer's tone, see his face, and feel my own discomfort.

1974

A final-year seminar on A PASSAGE TO INDIA, led by an American literary critic and young British historian who now teaches at one of the great American universities. The former asked me a complicated question about the politics of the book. I replied that Forster's obvious, but still covert, erotic interest in the untouchable youth in the courtroom scenes undermined, or even invalidated, whatever other social point he was making...

Still in the closet at the time, I was embarrassed to have brought up the subject - it still made me blush - but quite proud to have done so without being struck by lightning. Far from taking my point, the lecturers accused me of not listening to what was being said in class...My point was ignored. The questions was put to another student, and the discussion went off in the direction our tutors had preordained.

1977

I registered to write a Ph.D. thesis entitled "Male Homo-erotic Themes In Poetry In English, 1914-1980." After the first year's work, I presented my plans to a research committee, which had to approve what I was doing. The committee consisted of six male academics, at least one of them was gay.

1986

Chairing an undergraduate seminar on Augen's "Lay Your Sleeping Head, My Love," I withheld the information that the poet was gay until half an hour's discussion of his attitude to his "girlfriend" had taken place. When I asked, "If I told you he was homosexual, would you read it differently?" I heard the same answers which we had given to the same questions when I was a student. Nothing, it seemed, had changed.

1987

My Ph.D. thesis, rewritten, was published by Yale University Press...The Public Library orders were severely restricted by Margaret Thatcher's newly ratified homophobic law, Section 28 of the Local Government Act, which forbids the "promotion" of homosexuality by publicly funded bodies.

1989

A meeting of A-Level examiners in a London hotel. At lunch I sat opposite the most friendly and approachable of my fellow examiners, a middle-aged woman, who had shown in the meeting a range of humane and liberal attitudes to the students whose work we were reading, and a generous approach to assessment. Half-way through the meal, she asked about my SILENCE =DEATH lapel button. When I told her it was a slogan from the AIDS crisis, she asked in apparently genuine bewilderment, "Why are you interested in that?"

1990

A job interview at a college in the Midlands. This was the first time, in a decade of interviews, I have ever been asked about the relation between my gayness, my teaching and my students; the first time I have ever been treated as a whole professional, rather than as one who has a private life which he is allowing to seep dangerously into his teaching life. It does not seem insignificant that this interview panel consisted of three women and no men. I was offered the job...I am aware that things could have been much worse. I have never experienced violence, or lost a job (though I may have been denied several) because I was gay. I have had an easy ride...

1993

Tenure at last. For the first time in my career, no longer held back by short-term contracts. I have been able to start planning future courses in cultural studies: one on contemporary lesbian and gay cultures, another on representations of AIDS. For the first time eligible for a sabbatical, I can make longer-term research plans. For the first time eligible for promotion, I may eventually see my status catching up with my experience.

I have been involved in supervising lesbian and gay research by students on my own degree and exchange students from the United States. I am also, at last, starting to supervise a gay man's doctoral dissertation. This, I feel, is part of what I came into the profession to do.

On the negative side, however, I know that some senior staff were opposed to my being granted tenure because of the nature of my research interests. I know, too, that my employer once said that having me on the staff was like employing a religious fundamentalist. More depressingly for the first time in my career, I am occasionally encountering harassment from students when I raise lesbian or gay topics in lectures. To have a group of them slamming their notebooks shut and glaring at me while I speak is an unnerving experience, but is not a great trauma. In the end, the problem is theirs. I must conclude that we're moving in the right direction. The struggle continues, but at least I am now confronting it from a position of relative power. One can only hope that, in future, lesbian and gay academics will not have to wait so long before being taken seriously. Looking back on my career thus far, the best I can say is that homophobia has been wasting my time.

❖❖❖❖❖❖❖❖❖❖❖❖❖❖❖❖❖❖❖❖❖❖❖❖❖❖❖❖❖❖❖❖

About The Author

Gregory Woods ❖ *Gregory was born in Egypt in 1953. He teaches English , Literature and Creative Writing at Nottingham Polytechnic, England. He is the author of ARTICULATE FLESH: MALE HOMO-EROTICISM AND MODERN POETRY. He is currently writing a book on Marcel Proust. His first collection of poems, WE HAVE THE MELON, will be soon published.*

❖❖❖❖❖❖❖❖❖❖❖❖❖❖❖❖❖❖❖❖❖❖❖❖❖❖❖❖❖❖❖❖

❖❖❖❖❖❖❖❖❖

ABOUT THE PHOTOGRAPHER

Tam Garson ❖
*A certified
Veterinary
Technician and
free lance writer,
her photos have
been published
in veterinary
journals as well
as many lesbian
and gay publications.
She lives with her
lover, Tara and her
family of pets. Photo
inquiries welcome:
P.O. Box 3443
Enfield, Ct. 06083
-3443*

Man With Computer

photo by Tam Garson

"One does not have to be a lesbian, to read as a lesbian."
Excerpts from ON THE LINE radio show; interview with Joanne Glasgow and Karla Jay

Karla: I have had the experience, and I'm sure many have, of reading texts when I was in high school or college, and knowing that my own response was very different from everyone else's. Usually the professor, however, discounted the possiblity that the kind of reading I was giving this text could be right. Whether we are reading a lesbian text or not, we, as readers, bring our experiences to the page.

Joanne: Reader response is very important...

Host: What is meant by a lesbian text?

Karla: That's an extremely difficult question and I don't think there's any one answer to that. It could mean a book or text written BY a lesbian; it could also mean a book or text written ABOUT a lesbian. For example, in our latest publication, LESBIAN TEXTS AND CONTEXTS; RADICAL REVISIONS (NYU Press, 1990), Paula Bennett wrote an essay about Emily Dickinson, doing a reading of her poetry as a lesbian - the first such reading we've ever seen. Also, Marilyn Farwell shows in her reading of MISTS OF AVALON, which is certainly a heterosexual text with a heterosexual plot, that spaces exist where there is clearly erotic response between women.

Host: Does one have to be a lesbian to read as a lesbian?

Karla: No - a case in point, one does not have to be a 16th century white male to read Shakespeare (this is a highly political statement to make). Here, lesbians are putting lesbians at the center of the plot. In a sense, we as lesbians are the reading eye-I and we invite other people to come into our position. If it were not possible to read as a lesbian, so many "straight" people, like my students, would not be able to enjoy books like RUBYFRUIT JUNGLE...

❖❖❖

KARLA JAY is Associate Professor of English at Pace University, NYC and has coedited three anthologies with Allen Young, including OUT OF THE CLOSETS: VOICES OF GAY LIBERATION. Her most recent book, THE AMAZON AND THE PAGE: NATALIE CLIFFORD BARNEY AND RENEE VIVIAN, a biographical and literary study of two Paris expatriates.
JOANNE GLASGOW is a Professor of English at Bergen Community College, Paramus, N.J. and is past president and long-time officer of MLA Women's Caucus. Member of CUNY Lesbian and Gay Advisory Board.

❖❖❖

THE CLOSET AND THE CLASSROOM; *Reflections of an Aging Lesbian Professor*

by Virginia Ramey Mollenkott, Ph.D.

I am a lesbian woman who has been teaching college English since 1953, when I was 21 years old. For the first decade and a half, I taught in Protestant fundamentalist colleges that matched my religious background: Bob Jones University, Shelton College, Nyack College. In those places, because homosexuality was considered sinful, I had to keep my lesbianism secret on pain of immediate dismissal. The secret was easier to keep because I was married and eventually became a mother. But because I derived most of my emotional support from women, rumors abounded. At one point during my tenure at Shelton College on the Skylands campus in Ringwood, New Jersey, I would surely have been fired at the slightest hint of homosexuality. It was only my great popularity with the students that caused the administration to back off.

Being in the closet took a great toll emotionally, especially when I recognized that certain of my students were lesbian or gay, yet was not able to be frank with them about my orientation. In particular, I remember one young gay man at Nyack College who asked me how to get in touch with the New York gay community. In those days there were no hot lines and no Center to which people could be referred, but I told him as much as I dared. For many years afterwards, I prayed for that young man, feeling miserable about lacking the courage to tell him how much we had in common. But recently, when I was preaching at an Integrity service in New York City, I met the same man, no longer young but still very gay, who told me he was living happily in a long-term covenanted relationship. To my immense relief, he assured me that despite my inability to be open

21

with him, he had sensed my support and kinship and had remembered me as a good friend on his journey toward self-affirmation.

Things began to look up for me in 1967 when I commenced teaching at William Paterson College of New Jersey, got a divorce, bought a house with my partner, and began to venture out of the closet. I have never worn a sandwich sign proclaiming my orientation, but I have proceded to live my life openly and have refused ever to cave in to attempts at extortion. For instance, when my husband threatened to prove my lesbianism in court in order to gain custody of our son, I told him to do his damndest; and until our day in court, I was not certain whether or not he would make good on his threat. He didn't.

Later, when I received an anonymous note saying that the Dean of one of the schools at William Paterson College was telling people that I was lesbian, I took the note immediately to the Dean of the School of Humanities. When he said, "Oh, it would be horrible if this were true of you," I ignored the implied question and judgement, pointing out that the real issues were (1) who is writing anonymous notes? and (2) is the other Dean really making statements she has no business making? I insisted that we contact the other Dean then and there, and of course she fell all over herself denying that she had been issuing any such statements. I never found out who had typed the anonymous note but I didn't really care, knowing that my swift response had already delivered the message that I was not cowering in a closet and would not hesitate to fight for my human and professional rights.

I do a great deal of guest lecturing at religious colleges, churches, and conferences, and in 1983 decided to begin speaking openly about my lesbianism from the platform or pulpit. That decision also freed me to be more overtly talkative on campus, not simply advocating justice for lesbigay people as I had always done, but identifying myself as one of those for whom I was seeking justice. I have become very assertive about lesbigay rights at faculty meetings, especially the Race and Gender Faculty Seminars that eventually contributed to the development of the New Jersey

Project for transforming the curriculum in the direction of greater inclusiveness. For instance, when several faculty members gave presentations to the Seminar concerning the ways they have introduced feminist, race and class issues into their courses, I objected strenuously that they had not included gay and lesbian issues as well. One of the panelists, Robert Rosen, had the good grace to admit that I was right; and I notice that the anthology he subsequently edited presents lesbian and gay writers with calm explicitness about their sexuality. I recommend this book warmly as a model of curriculum transformation at its best: LITERATURE AND SOCIETY: AN INTRODUCTION TO FICTION, DRAMA, NONFICTION, edited by Pamela J. Annas and Robert C. Rosen (Englewood Cliffs: Prentice Hall, 1990). We need to let publishers know that we appreciate books like this one!

During the past several years, a Coalition of Gays, Lesbians, and their Friends has been organized among the students at William Paterson College. I have tried to attend Coalition meetings at least once each semester, encouraging those who attend to pass the word on the grapevine that I am lesbian and would welcome lesbian and gay in my classes, whether or not they wish to be open about their orientation. But if they wish to be open, I am glad to provide a forum in which they can speak and write freely about what it's like to be lesbian or gay in American society. I also participate in on-campus panel discussions, for instance identifying myself as a lesbian in a panel on spirituality and taking part in a well-attended panel on lesbian lives. Many students are also aware that I have entered testimony as an expert religious witness on behalf of A-634, New Jersey's lesbian and gay rights protection bill.

I have spent a lot of time thinking about whether to mention my being a lesbian in my own English literature and writing classes. Of course I have never missed an opportunity to advocate justice for lesbians and gay men, and have been careful to be explicit about lesbigay points of view. When I am teaching an author who was or is gay or lesbian, I include that fact among other facts that help to illuminate what she or he is all about.

And if students protest that sexual orientation is irrelevant, as one student did concerning the nineteenth gay Jesuit poet Gerard Manley Hopkins, that simply opens the class for discussion of the fact that orientation goes far beyond genital activity to include a person's whole way of being in the world.

But as of the date of this writing, I have never stated in one of my classes that I am a lesbian woman. Here are my reasons: students are often placed into classes by computer, or are forced to take certain classes because of curricular or scheduling constraints. And within the classroom walls, there is a power differential based on the fact that the teacher has the gradebook and the students need decent grades in order to proceed toward graduation. Therefore I hesitate to tell my students something they should hear only in a context (such as the panel on lesbian lives) where they will not be distracted by fears based on stereotypes. For instance, if I should casually mention my being a lesbian in an English class (without explanation of the complexities of sexual orientation that are really not appropriate in such classes) there are sure to be a few young men who would fear that my lesbianism means I hate men and therefore them, and a few young women who would fear they might have to sleep with me to get a good grade.

On the other hand, how will such stereotypes ever be broken down if the students never realize that some of their most popular and respected teachers are lesbian or gay? My own policy so far has been to be as public as possible about my lesbianism on the campus in the more extra-curricular settings, in the hope that those people who need to know I am there will get the message. When I have eventually come out to certain individual students, I have asked them whether they were aware I was lesbian before I told them. So far, the hetereosexual students have said they were not aware, but that they knew I was committed to justice for everyone and also that they could tell me anything about themselves without shocking me. The gay men or lesbian women are sometimes aware, either because of the grapevine or their own instincts; but those who are surprised at my news say that it was OK not to know for sure because what they DID know was the important thing - that they would be valued, included, and affirmed in my classes.

Often when I am talking in my classes about gay or lesbian issues, I find myself wondering why everyone seems so relaxed and agreeable, why no one is saying anything heterosexist or homophobic. It occurs to me that perhaps the students in this particular class have finally gotten the word that I am lesbian. But when I ask individual trusted students whether that is the case, the answer is always the same: no, it's just that you are so relaxed and comfortable with the topic that everybody else feels relaxed as well. The same thing happens at church conferences: although not every agrees that gay is good, the atmosphere tends to stay calm and open. So there must be real validity to the observation that the comfort-level of the speaker tends to affect the comfort-level of those who listen and respond.

Recently I lectured on homosexuality at a very conservative college in the Midwest. I had been warned that the students were from extremely right-wing backgrounds and had never heard public discussion of homosexuality on campus, so there was bound to be some hostile questioning. But it never happened. There were plenty of questions, some of them betraying vast ignorance but none of them betraying hostility. Afterwards the resident faculty expressed amazement at the calmness of the atmosphere; but I have witnessed the same phenomenon again and again, whenever the teacher, speaker, or facilitator is confident of the facts, comfortable talking about them, and peacefully self-accepting.

I have concluded that the most important thing teachers can do to help young people grow into just-minded and reasonable adults is to become completely comfortable with themselves, including their own sexuality. Whether or not teachers are lesbigay and whether or not we are free to mention it, we are transmitting an important message simply by advocating justice for all people, in a quiet and relaxed manner. If getting to that point requires some psychotherapy, teachers should invest in it. If it requires hard study of intelligent religious, phychological, or medical approaches to

25

sexuality, then the time and energy will be well spent. The goal, after all, is a world in which every person would be supported in becoming all that they were meant to be - soaring as high as possible, but always on their own wings.

❖❖❖❖❖❖❖❖❖❖❖❖❖❖❖❖❖❖❖❖❖❖❖❖❖❖❖❖❖❖❖❖❖

Virginia Ramey Mollenkott, Ph.D. ❖ *Teaches English at the college level, writes books and enjoys gardening, swimming, and good conversation. She also lectures widely and is a member of Women of Faith (an inter-religious dialogue group), and various lesbigay and professional organizations. Serves on the Board of Directors of Kirkridge Conference Center; Pacem in Terris; and the Upper Room AIDS Ministry.*

❖❖❖❖❖❖❖❖❖❖❖❖❖❖❖❖❖❖❖❖❖❖❖❖❖❖❖❖❖❖❖❖❖

BOOK REVIEW
by Sue McConnell-Celi

SENSUOUS SPIRITUALITY: Out From Fundamentalism
Virginia Ramey Mollenkott
Crossroad Press, New York, 1992

Imagine says the author, you are on a Futuristic Board of Planners to set forth the moral and ethical rules for a society into which you are to be born. You have no knowledge of your gender, color, sexual orientation, mental/physical capabilities, socio-economic status or whether your nation is powerful or weak. What Bible passages would you be most likely to emphasize? ...These are just a few of the questions posed in SENSUOUS SPIRITUALITY: Out From Fundamentalism, along with discourse reflecting both the external and internal blockages that have disallowed so many from enjoying full religious and social participation.

Virginia Ramey Mollenkott, an English professor at William Paterson College, Wayne, New Jersey, has authored seven books, including IS THE HOMOSEXUAL MY NEIGHBOR? and THE DIVINE FEMININE. In her latest, she lives up to her usual high standards. While weaving connections between biblical, classical and contemporary, the cachet of her writings, she lessens the chasm between the sensual and spiritual, the inner person and the outer world. In doing so, she demonstrates the irrationality of forfeiting physical love for spiritual life, and vice versa, providing a message society may sorely need. But women especially have been harmed by society's double standard, one that has indeed defiled sexuality.

For that reason, it seems appropriate that a lesbian feminist address this topic, whose concepts reinforce a positive view of women - in this reviewer's opinion, nearly paralleling the affirmations and empowerment held in Tantric rituals and matriarchal cultures of old - yet she observes that ALL people - lesbigays (lesbians, bisexuals and gays) and heterosexuals have suffered under the enforced, religiously backed system of HETEROPATRIARCHY...Instead, Mollenkott suggests, why not turn away from patriarchy towards partnership? One worthy solution rests with the lesbigay community, whose relationships go beyond social overlays and conventions, comprising not "just matters of what you do in bed," but rather, wedges that pry open new spaces, making room for more integrated, total human beings, and therefore a more unified society. One avenue toward full integration is the use of the senses, and in particularly TOUCH, which not only heals, but connects the body to the spirit...she encourages "more functional church families...not only nuclear families, but singles with or without children, intergenerational families, multicurtural adoptive families, gay or lesbian couples, and so forth so that simply by learning to care for each other, cluster members would be learning to honor diversity...

Does SENSUOUS SPIRITUALITY accomplish (its mission)? Undoubtedly. As the reader journeys through these twelve chapters ranging from "Gender Constructs and the Human Imaging of God" to the ethics of silence, passing and outing, - she (Mollenkott uses the generic feminine throughout, notice HE is already included in that pronoun) will get more than a glimpse of life beyond the HETEROSEXIST GLASS CAGE in a psychological first step towards transforming society.
(Reprinted from NETWORK and SAPPHO'S ISLE)

26

CROSSROADS: TURNING POINT FOR A FOURTH GRADE TEACHER *by Gil Burgess* *

Crossroads, Forks in the Road, Turning Points, no matter what you call it, we all make decisions. Life itself is a series of decisions, ranging from what to eat for dinner to what tie to wear to finding a life-mate.

I recently found myself at one of life's crossroads. Before I decided upon which path to follow, however, I evaluated and carefully judged the immediate and long range results that could occur. Before I begin, though, remember no decision is 100%, and that only hindsight is 20/20.

◆◆◆◆◆◆◆◆◆◆◆◆◆◆◆◆◆◆◆◆◆◆◆◆◆

I have never been one to hide my sexuality; I'm gay...so what! I am still a person with rights. The right to speak my mind, hold a job of my choice, and love whom I choose. I am also a teacher, and I hope that through my "Life Lessons," as my former students call them, I can enlighten just a few children to be less judgemental and more accepting when they reach adulthood. I realize that our society is not utopia, least of all for gay men and lesbians.

Through of series of events that are not relevant here, I was asked to be interviewed for an article on Gays and Lesbians. I

* Originally, the author of this article wanted anonymity; however, now he writes: "After much thought and debate, I have decided that my name MAY be used. Thank you for using my story."

was anxious to participate, glad for the opportunity to give the straight community a "Life Lesson". The interview went well. We covered a variety of topics. After it was over, I felt good; I believed my comments, along with those of other interviewees, would present an honest, well balanced summary of our culture.

Then I came to my Crossroad. The reporter asked, "Can we use your real name?"

Immediately, I saw street signs of my two paths, "Yes Blvd" and "No Way", but I couldn't see very far either path. I was unsure, but, at the same time proud of MY words and tentatively answered, "Yes".

Over the next few days, I mentally "walked" a ways down both paths, weighing the results along each.

Along the "No Way" I saw lots of notoriety and praise.

Along "Yes Blvd" I came upon ridicule, harassment, discrimination, possible job loss.

If I stayed with my 'yes' decision, would I be able to continue my "Life Lessons" and attain my goals?

If I changed to a "no" decision, would I be hypocritical?

As the rush of being interviewed for a newspaper article faded, I came to a realization that changed my confusion to clarity - it doesn't matter WHO says these things, just as long as they are said!

Along about this same time, I was in contact with my Association president concerning the National Education Association Convention to which I had just been elected a delegate. I told her about the article and my dilemma. Before I could tell her of my final decision, she responded by saying, "I know you won't like this, but I'd like you NOT to use your real name. Your job could be on the line and you could do more for gay and lesbian students by staying in the system."

"You're right," I responded, "I don't like it, but I agree. Thanks."

With the realization that "I" was not the focal point of the article and the conversation with my Association president, I was now able to confidently travel down one path, that of "No Way" without further question.

YOUR BOARD OF EDUCATION ELECTION

Leonard Green's excerpts from CAPITAL SPOTLIGHT, Washington, DC

...Lesbians and gay men are taxpayers, therefore our opinions are essential in any public process to appoint a person to a position or to elect someone to public office. We have the moral, political and economic right to request that the public system examine its selection carefully of the next superintendent...As an African-American gay strategist and gayologist, I am concerned about all students receiving proper education and guidance. More specifically, I am concerned about gay and lesbian youth within the public school system receiving sufficient support from educators who must assist all students in understanding sexual orientation. Children's education is at hand here, not some pretext for preferential treatment. Administrators, teachers and the like must understand that sensitive programs must be put in place to educate people about homosexuality as it relates to gay and lesbian youth...

❖❖❖❖❖❖❖❖❖❖❖❖❖❖❖❖❖❖❖❖❖❖❖❖❖❖❖❖❖

Leonard Green

Former president of the Langston and Jones Society, New Orleans. Leonard has been active in many activities including: Project Director of New Orleans Health Department AIDS program, alternate delegate to the 1990 National Gay Republican Convention, radio host and DC Coalition of Black Lesbians and Gay Men.

photo by Jason Niccolo Johnson

"DEFERRING TO WHAT IS PERCEIVED AS HETEROSEXUAL ENTITLEMENT"

author requests anonymity

We buried my lover's grandmother today, a very atypical Halloween, warm, sunny, and dry. The last several months had been consumed with walking across the park to the hospital, watching her fight for breath, the struggle for life. So when my lover's mother came over to tell us the news, she put her arms around us and described how it was for her to watch her mother die.

In the half hour commute to the school where I teach, I am transformed into another, a teacher. I have always loved the time to commute across the plains, it's a way to change from lesbian to teacher and back again every day. But today, Halloween, my identities merge uncomfortably as I realize I just can't get dressed up as a skeleton or a ghost, and face a room full of excited ten-year-olds carving pumpkins, bobbing for apples, and eating too much candy.

They ask about my costume, where is it? I respond that my costume is this dress I'm wearing, they're unfamiliar wnough with seeing me in a skirt, so I hope this will satisfy them. I make an attempt at a more honest explanation. I'm going to a friend's funeral this afternoon kids, and I just feel too sad to dress up, someone else will take over this afternoon.

Okay, no problem, they are consumed with Halloween, and I'm present for the party, acting as though nothing is wrong, after all, I'm in that compartment of my life where nothing IS wrong. I smile and I've kept them happy.

I rehearse what I will tell my principal:

My lover's grandmother died and I need this afternoon off to attend the funeral. I have to admit I'm really upset, I've never even seen a dead person before last night. I'm really struggling with the finality of death.

My friend's grandmother...
My roommate's grandmother...
My own grandmother?
My friend died...
I'm going to a funeral this afternoon.

31

I settled on the last one, it was short, sweet, to the point with little revelation of myself, that's definately the one that best suits me.

The family rides in the limo, her parents, sister, brother, his girlfriend, my partner and I. As we approach the graveside, I assess the situation quickly, seven people, six chairs. As people are filing in to sit, I automatically step behind the chairs, instantly thinking, "Why did I do that? Why did I think her brother's girlfriend was able to sit there by her partner and not me?"

That is one of the things that still haunts me. The way I automatically defer to what I perceive to be heterosexual entitlement. The way I reflexively step back, give up my power, and allow straight couples validity and let my relationship take a back seat. I attempt not to blame myself, pledge not to defer the next opportunity, for there are always more chances to grow.

It's difficult to look at the society in which I live and not be angry. I love my job, but it necessitates hiding so much of myself. There are people at work that have no clue that I'm a lesbian, and I see their looks when I discuss painting my own house, fixing my own garbage disposal, or traveling. How sad, they think that I must do these things alone! As I go through major life crises and major changes for the best, my school friends are unaware. I have known most of these people for fifteen years. Fifteen years ago, I was a straight woman wanting a career and children; now I'm a lesbian, growing in my relationship more and more as each year passes. In the last fifteen years, I've separated from my family of origin, cared for a disabled lover for years, and settled into a life partnership where I can't imagine being happier. Yet, my colleagues see the same old me.

I often hear the argument that if everyone would "come out", discrimination would have come to an end. I find this an oversimplification because the world doesn't change because I want it to, the power to change is an inside job.

Sometimes I resent the energy spent all day, every day not to make certain waves, or "offend" people, or be offended by people - I wonder about the effect this has on my lover and me. Everyday I fear someone will recognize that I'm a lesbian, and I fear no one will. Also...the seat at the funeral WAS intended for me.

❖❖❖

The Author : "I teach all subjects in upper elementary grades, and I'm 38 years old. In addition to teaching, I facilitate support groups for children, and for adults who are dealing with grief. I love walking my dog, reading, gardening, and spending time with my partner." (This article was written in 1990. Today the author, who lives in Colorado, writes: "This (topic) is very important given the political climate in Colorado at the present time."

❖❖❖

HIGH SCHOOL GYM TEACHER GRANTED BEREAVEMENT LEAVE

One LAGE member reports she was automatically granted bereavement leave when her lover of 12 years died. "I work with great people who have known us for years, inviting both of us to their houseparties and special events. We have mutual respect for each other professionally and personally. I can't imagine any one of them being malicious, especially in my time of grief."

LAGE: Lesbian and Gay Educators of N.J.

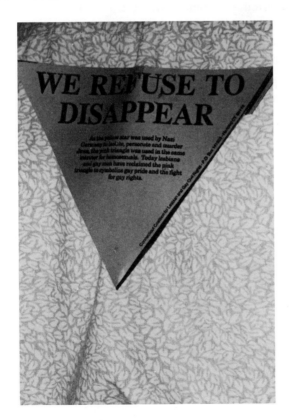

"We Refuse To Disappear"

photo by Tam Garson

COMING OUT - AS A TEACHER

by Henry D. Robertson

I have been very interested in the controversy concerning the "outing" of closet lesbians and gays in America. It has made me reflect on some of my own experiences when I made a personal decision to come out of the closet at a time when I had been for twenty years Head of English in a London comprehensive school.

I would point out that this preceded Section 28 and when the still-extant ILEA was promoting an anti-sexist, anti-racist campaign, which, for the most part, had my support. After all, while being raised in Scotland, I was brought up on the simple but generously humane philosophy: "We're a' Jock Tamson's bairns" and on the poems of Robert Burns.

I personally considered anti-racism and anti-sexism as rather limiting, since they were negative concepts. I felt that it was much more important to provide my pupils (who were from fifty-two different countries of origin) with positive images - of writers from a variety of racial backgrounds, of women and of lesbians and gay men. So, as a Department, we ordered books James Baldwin and V S Naipaul in addition to those we already had by the Brontes and Oscar Wilde.

This ILEA policy by itself was not the thing which made me

"come out" and present myself as, I hope, a positive image of an openly gay person.

To fill in the background: a couple of years before, as a result of my anger at Customs and Excise raiding Gay's The Word Bookshop, I decided to go on my very first Gay Pride March. I went by tube to the gathering-point at Marble Arch and wore a paper sticker on my lapel which bore the pink triangle and gave the date and place of the march. As tube-travellers are generally totally impassive, I did not realise that my sticker had registered with any of them. At Bond Street Station, three youths got up to leave the train. The last one of them turned round at the door, spat at me and shouted: "Queer - ----!" He stepped outside, the door slid to and the train was off.

I was staggered by my own reaction. I think that, once upon a time, I might have curled up and died of shame and embarassment - but this time, I felt such towering superiority over anyone who could behave in such a way, that I determined to nail my colours to the mast-head and continue to wear the triangle, without letting someone else control my actions. There are lots of good reasons to dislike me but to hate me on sight because of my being gay is unworthy of any thinking human being. In a sense, I felt grateful for the experience, since it gave me an insight into how Jews and Black people must have felt in similar circumstances.

So I began to wear a metal pink triangle at school, as well as everywhere else. For the most part, I must say, I had a fairly easy ride, with some amusing moments on the way.

Although sporting the pink triangle might be seen as an act of bold defiance, it wasn't really, because I soon began to realise that practically nobody knows what it means.

School-kids, though, are interested in badges and so, occasionally, in the course of a lesson, a pupil would ask what it signified.

"It means that I'm gay," I would answer.

It was often quite amusing to see the stunned look on the pupil's face as he shook his head, as if surely he had mis-heard me and repeated the question. When I explained further that the badge was a version of that worn by the homosexuals gassed in Hitler's concentration camps, for the most part, they seemed shocked...

There was a very small boy of twelve whom I had often seen about the school with his thumb in his mouth and big eyes like headlamps. Once when we were alone on the same staircase, he took his thumb out of his mouth and said: "Are you gay, sir?"

"Yes."

He took his thumb out again and said, "What does 'gay' mean, sir?"

For a minute, I thought he was pretending ignorance (after all this was the 1990's), till I looked at his deeply furrowed brow.

I said, "You'll understand when you're a bit older."

He was quite determined, though, and persisted with: "but what do you do, sir?"

"I teach English in Room 28," I said as I swept up the staircase.

The boy was very persistent, though, and approached me once again, this time in the playground, asking where he could buy a pink badge. When I asked why he wanted it, he said,

"Because it's pretty, sir."

In my best dominie-style, I raged, "But you don't wear a badge like this because it's pretty - you've got to earn it!"

There were nastier occasions, as when the newspaper's "gay plague" campaign was on. Some of the more senior boys would very elaborately press their backs against the wall as I passed by.

When a more senior boy called, "Queer!" after me, I reported it to the deputy headmaster and I was impressed by the support I had from my colleagues...

I saw myself as being a "positive image", always assuming that there were gay and lesbian pupils in my classes, but none of them every confided in me that they were. I do hope those who were there took heart from acquaintance with a teacher who was known to be gay and proud of it. For the most part, I was impressed by how accepting my pupils were of my "coming out". They left me with the feeling that, were it not for the policy of the more contemptible tabloids, anti-gay prejudice would fall into decline.

But to return to forcing people "out" - I can see why people might want to do such a thing in dealing with gay and lesbian people who actively support anti-gay measures but I do not consider that it is something to be done indiscriminately. I myself came out, after long reflection, in a work-place where I had been established for years, and in the full knowledge of having a sufficiently large and reliable body of friends - and colleagues - to support me if things got rough.

(This article appeared in *Gay Scotland Magazine*)

❖❖❖❖❖❖❖❖❖❖❖❖❖❖❖❖❖❖❖❖❖❖❖❖❖❖❖❖❖❖

About the Author

Henry D. Robertson ❖ *Was raised in Aberdeen. He graduated with an MA (Hons) and taught Language and Literature in secondary schools in Scotland before going to work for six years in a British Army boarding school in Germany. In 1965, he came to London as Head of English in a comprehensive school and remained on that post until the age of 60. Henry enjoys reading, photography, cinema, the theatre and performing with the Gay Drama Workshop.*

❖❖❖❖❖❖❖❖❖❖❖❖❖❖❖❖❖❖❖❖❖❖❖❖❖❖❖❖❖❖

The Oscar Wilde Memorial Bookshop Ad Logo

THE LABRYS
Double-Headed axe of ancient warriors. Symbol of Lesbian-Feminist strength and struggle. We wear it now express our Lesbian Pride.

THE PINK TRIANGLE
In the Nazi concentration camps, Gay Men were forced to wear pink triangle patches on their clothing. We wear it today as a symbol of Gay Resistance.

(Oscar Wilde Bookshop of NYC)

GAY/STRAIGHT: AN ALLIANCE FOR HIGH SCHOOL ACTIVISM
by Nancy Boutilier

Imagine signs hanging in the halls of your high school proclaiming "Gay Awareness Week." Each day, photographs and short biographies of famous gay men and lesbians appear on the wall: Alvin Ailey and Rita Mae Brown on Monday. Audre Lorde and Paul Monette on Tuesday. Martina Navratilova and Tennessee Williams on Wednesday, and so on.

Imagine ninth graders reading Larry Kramer's play THE NORMAL HEART for English class. Discussion begins with a young girl raising her hand to ask: "Is there such a thing as a lady homosexual?"

Imagine twelfth graders reading Rita Mae Brown's novel RUBYFRUIT JUNGLE alongside JANE EYRE. When asked to write comments and questions on the blackboard to spark classroom discussion, the students chalk an extensive list that includes the following queries to their classmates:

"Isn't everyone bisexual?"

"Why does Molly Bolt have to go to 'some branch of hell' to find herself? Is society so close-minded and truly unwilling to change?"

One boy claims, "Molly could have good sex with a guy, but probably just hasn't found a good one." Someone else's response: "Does that mean every man can have good sex with another man, if he finds the right one?"

Imagine a morning in which every tenth mailbox in the school is stuffed with a pink paper triangle stamped "One In Ten." By lunchtime, the school newspaper carries a letter to the editor beginning: "How many of you got a pink triangle in your mailbox this week? How many of you know someone who did?" The letter goes on to explain the meaning of 'one in ten' and outlines the historical significance of the pink triangle from Nazi concentration camps to ACT-UP. The letter is signed by ten people, students and faculty members, declaring themselves members of the Gay/Straight Alliance.

Imagine a visit to your school from the president. About eighty students line the motorcade with protest signs. Amid "My Body, My Choice" and "Fight Racism" signs, large pink triangles urge "Gay Rights" and remind the president that "Silence Hurts." He smiles and waves as his limousine speeds past the demonstrators and their signs, the crowd attending the event is witness to the students' commitment to gay and lesbian rights. The six o'clock news offers viewers across New England a glimpse of the students' efforts as television stations split coverage of the event between two stories - the president and the protesters.

Are you also imagining the outrage and backlash these occurances might provoke? Angry letters to school administrators? A call for teacher firings? Gay and lesbian visibility in high schools across America can be risky business, but the scenes above are more than dreamy imaginings. They are already moments in history, the history of a people at one school, pointing to change and furnishing hope for the future. I wish I could write a "How-To" manual that would guarantee everyone working for lesbian and gay visibility as much professional reward and personal growth as I experienced at Phillips Academy, the prep school in Andover, Massachusetts where I taught English for five years.

Unfortunately, any pre-packaged program offered for universal application would foolishly overlook the importance of context. The private meetings, public activities and curriculum developments that took place while I was at Phillips Academy reflect both a bold, heroic valor and a timid discretion (often said to be the better half of valor). Progress was certainly made, but not always in the most logical or time-expedient fashion. Decisions were made both with regard for the needs of the group as a whole and with respect for the needs of group members.

This is the story of a coalition building that went into the founding of the Phillips Academy Gay/Straight Alliance and the collective effort that emerged triumphantly from that group. The gains in gay and lesbian visibility have occurred as a result of the consultation and compromise of many individuals working together within a particular context. Efforts to bring gay and lesbian issues into the school's consciousness were successful, in part, because we were able to focus on our common ground - a shared commitment to fight homophobia. The group - which included individuals identifying themselves as bisexual, straight, gay, and lesbian - gained the respect of the larger campus community, in part as a result of the trust and admiration group members showed for one another, and because of our efforts to nurture inclusiveness. Within the group, we strove to celebrate our differences rather than allowing them to divide us, and individual decisions regarding how "out" one chose "to be or not to be" were respected and supported by those chosing differently.

At best, details of our story provide concrete ideas for promoting gay and lesbian visibility in other settings. The public events are tangible evidence of the empowerment that followed the formation of a small support group that met weekly out of the public eye. Particular agenda items often had to wait for students and teachers to grow in trust of one another, but we did learn to support each other. Discovering acceptance within the group empowered individuals to walk more comfortable in the larger community knowing that the collective strength of the group walked alongside. As individuals grew stronger, the group chose to shift some of its attention from the inner work to raising the consciousness level of the community.

Because the focus of change was often on visibility, the story of my own coming out is threaded through this narrative. Individual journeys often became part of the group's journey, and likewise, the group's actions often marked personal milestones. If I seem vague in reference to a given "we," it is out of respect for the privacy of others and also to acknowledge the supremely collaborative dimensions of these efforts. Unfortunately, such usage tends to erase any voice of dissent that rose up in the process of arriving at consensus. Trust me, we, those of us who emerged as active members did NOT always agree on how to move forward, but we managed to keep together - sometimes creeping along and sometimes sprinting.

THE BEGINNING

We call ourselves the Gay/Straight Alliance because we are all working together to make Phillips Academy as safe and as comfortable a place to be gay, lesbian, or bisexual as it is to be heterosexual. We are working to end homophobia as a step toward furthering the appreciation of the diversity on this campus and a stance against an oppression which prohibits individuals from being the whole human beings that they are.

This self-definition, as it appeared in the school paper in May 1990, is not where we began. The first meeting of what would become the Gay/Straight Alliance occurred on February 7, 1989 as a result of a short notice in the daily announcements: "Meeting to discuss homophobia. Tonight in Room 6 at 6:45. Everyone welcome."

Everyone was welcome, but we had no idea what we'd do if a hostile crowd showed up. A single beginning is impossible to pinpoint because a "we" existed prior to that first meeting. Plenty of consultation took place behind closed and often closeted doors. The name of the "Gay/Straight Alliance" was appropriate to the group even before the students chose it. The faculty "we" included two straight deans, Cilla and Pam, who had a great deal of credibility working with "the underbelly" of the school - drug and alcohol programs, sex education seminars and counseling. They had been instrumental in designing the AIDS education program with attention to issues of homophobia. The gay half of the faculty allegiance consisted of Kathy, coach and athletic administrator, and me. Neither one of us felt good about our closet status on campus, but we were convinced that professional survival depended on it. We both had colleagues whom we were out to, but personal survival depended heavily on our support of one another.

The fifth person of the "we," and the greatest catalyst for it all, was one eleventh grade girl who identified herself as a lesbian. An excellent student, Sharon was shy, withdrawn, and feeling alone in her self-knowledge. She was haunted by the isolation and the sense of hypocrisy

42

that accompanies life in the closet. She had passed on her intentions to start a gay support group to Cilla, the dean, who, in turn, looked for advice from her two favorite lesbians.

Cilla's consultations probably extend beyond my knowledge of her networking. When she told me that a student hoped to start a support group, my stomach cartwheeled with both fear and excitement. It took me only one guess to arrive at Sharon's name.

Two years earlier, before I ever heard anyone suggest that gay and lesbian students might benefit from a support group or role models, Sharon had been a ninth-grader in my English class. We read Homer's ODYSSEY, and when I asked students to write about the different kinds of heroes different cultures have. Sharon's essay contended that ours was a culture without any real life heroes. She listed famous and no-so-famous people whose imperfections had tainted their images in her eyes. Then she tossed the entire argument into my lap with the concluding question "How can a hero be someone who smokes marijauna or is a homosexual?"

The voice on the page seemed so desperate and disillusioned that I contemplated my response for quite a while. I had always been the drug-free type, and, at the time, I had only dated men in search of Mr. Right. I penned back in the margin "Or how about a homosexual who smokes marijuana?! How do these inhibit one's ability to give support to a friend, compassion to a stranger, or vision to a nation?"

Not long after articulating such open-mindedness in response to that journal entry, my life changed when I got involved, for the first time, with a woman. Then, about a year after my own coming out, I strutted along in my first Boston Gay Pride March, only to be greeted by that same student whose journal had forced me to rethink heroism. "What are you doing here?" Sharon asked. Now, with the clarity of hindsight, I see how closely my ability to articulate acceptance of homosexuality to a student was linked to my ability to accept my own feelings for women. I suppose I should have thanked her for raising the question when she did, but at the time, all I could do was mutter "I'm kind of into this stuff," as I pointed to my pins and the pink triangles draped over my dog.

Sharon and a friend had read about the parade in the paper. "Have you ever been in a group of gay people?" I asked. "Nope," they shook their heads revelling in amazement at "how many," "how normal everyone looks," "how is all of this kept so secret?" The questions rolled my way, and I answered to the best I could. Sharon had read a great deal about being gay, and I marvelled at how certain and secure she seemed about her own sexuality. That she saw me as a role model pleased me, but I was terrified to think what it meant for a student to possess my secret.

In September, Sharon and I greeted one another with a knowing nod, but we kept a distance between us that was formal and uncomfortable. I tried once to open the door for discussion by telling her, "If you ever want to talk about the march..." but I left it to her to initiate further conversation. Two years after reading her journal and within a year of marching beside her in the Gay Pride March, it was hardly a guess when I asked if Sharon was the one organizing a gay and lesbian support group. I told Cilla to count me in, I'd go the the meetings, but I didn't feel ready to come out to a group. She tended to agree, and reminded me that I had a great deal more to lose than the students. Cilla asked Sharon if she could mention the plan to "a gay faculty member," and it was hardly a guess when Sharon asked if I was the one.

Since Sharon had already seen beyond my ambiguity, I didn't want her to feel betrayed or let down by me if I didn't come out at meetings. She and I met to discuss the project and I told her then I wouldn't come out publicly unless I felt there was need for it, meaning if folks came to harass her. I wanted to assure her that I was proud to be a lesbian, and that she should not see my silence as shame. She said she understood, and she meant it, but I felt some discomfort and hypocrisy in it all. I was willing to stand with her, if and only if, provoked. She, on the other hand, felt so strongly about being seen for who she was that she was willing to stand alone and bear the consequences of other people's ignorance and fears.

44

She had a courage that I did not have. I could help word bulletin board announcements and provide resources, but she was the one risking most, the role model, the teacher; I was the one who would learn by her example.

On the Friday following that first meeting, a letter addressed to the editor of the school paper appeared under the headline "Homophobia":

Last Tuesday evening fifteen people met to discuss a topic that is too often ignored here at Phillips Academy. Unlike racism and sexism, nobody talks about homophobia. About ten percent of the population is homosexual, and, yes, there are homosexuals at this school. It's easy for most people to go through life laughing at all the gay jokes. It's not easy for those of us who are gay to hear our friends and classmates laugh at us or call us sick, insane, or worthy of being shot.

Sharon, and Sharon alone, chose to publicly allude to her own lesbian identity in full view of the campus community. I remember bracing myself everyday for the worst. I was prepared to stand with her, to play the trump card of coming out publicly if Sharon met with harassment. In the long run, this willingness may have helped as I eased out of the closet. In private, I half-wished that someone would launch a campaign against us that would spur me to come out once in my own self-righteousness defense. But I knew the less confrontation, the better for the students, both in the group and not in the group.

OUTER PATHS TO OUR BEGINNING

As is often the case with history, our documented memory has its unrecorded roots buried in oral history. Whatever acceptance and status Sharon and our group gained on campus, we owe credit, in part, to those who came before with their own courage that helped prepare the campus for our organization. I know at least one public such wave maker who left us smoother sailing in his wake. It took place a year before Sharon's activism when the entire class of four-hundred seniors had been assembled by their own student leaders to discuss the rise of racial tension on campus.

The hottest gossip buzzing in every campus corner the next morning was about the testimony given by one particular white student. In town meeting fashion, students took turns listing grievances, offering suggestions, asking questions. Eventually, a young man stood before his peers to call attention to the harassment he had received. "I know some of you think I'm gay," he announced and paused. "Well, I am." Another pause and plenty of silent tension in the crowded gym. "But that's not MY problem," he continued. "Unfortunately, some of you don't know how to deal with who I am, and if you can't deal with my being gay, that's your problem, not mine." After recovering their collective breath, the senior class rose around him, in admiration and, perhaps, apology, to applaud their gay classmate with a standing ovation. Although the drama of the moment may be lost in my telling of it, the power of his proclamation is reflected by the response of an African-American student in my class who said of the incident: "I went into that meeting thinking I had so much to teach the white kids, and I came out of there blown away by how much I had to learn."

THE STEPS WE TOOK

Our weekly attendance fluctuated, but meetings were advertised regularly and a core group of about ten people emerged. The group included gay, lesbian, bisexual and straight, male and female, from among the student body, faculty and staff. In the first year, probably two dozen individuals attended our meetings at different times. As the group grew more and more comfortable discussing issues, the more accurately meeting announcements reflected our agenda. We no longer advertised discussions of "homophobia," choosing to be as affirmative as possible with notices like "a supportive environment for talking about gay issues."

Certain aspects of the school aided our efforts. Boarding schools have flexible schedules. We had access to school vans for group outings to Gay Rights rallies and lectures in the city. We met between dinner and study hours once a week in a faculty member's on-campus home. We could show films and provide reading materials without fear of censorship. The meetings were off the beaten track but well publicized. Anyone who wanted to participate had to make a conscious effort. All were welcome, but only the interested found their way to us. We were able to achieve privacy without having to feel hidden; members who later joined us said the hardest part was not finding the meeting, but "getting up the courage."

Since boarding schools have an obligation to the personal lives of their students, faculty members are expected to give a listening ear to concerns and questions about stress, eating disorders, homework, family situations, drug and alcohol issues, and, yes, sexuality. Furthermore, the Gay/Straight Alliance was not the first minority group to call campus attention to overlooked needs. A school that thrived for over a century as an all-male, predominately white, well-to-do prep school, Phillips Academy is still in the process of discovering ramifications of coeducation and multiculturalism. By successfully organizing on campus, the Afro/Latino-American Student Association, the Asian Society, the Jewish Student Union and the Women's Forum have all preceded the Gay/Straight alliance in demonstrating how benefical support groups can be to individuals who view themselves marginalized by the campus mainstream.

On campus, as well as in cities across the US, gay and lesbian rights are being acknowledged today, in part, because other groups have come before to demand inclusion in social and political institutions. Although some folks at the academy might have preferred later to sooner, most saw the emergence of our group as a step whose time had come. A few years later, the school's disciplinary code included a policy against racism and sexism; we requested the policy be extended to specifically include homophobic harassment. When the school newspaper editor invited a half dozen student leaders to question candidates from candidates' night panel prior to student elections, the President of the Gay/Straight Alliance sat shoulder to shoulder with the five other student leaders. When a committee established a day of workshops for the observance of Martin Luther King Day, the theme "Striving For Peace," left us room to host a session: "Homophobia is Hatred Too," featuring THE TIMES OF HARVEY MILK. ...We called our straight comrades "homospirituals" and "homosocials" to emphasize commonality.

47

WHERE I STOOD

After a couple of months, the discussion group applied for official club status. The school required a president, and Sharon was elected with little debate. She orchestrated in as non-hierarchical a fashion as I've ever seen succeed at a high school level. By about the third meeting, I had come out to the group...The seniors in the group laughed at me when I suggested that some students didn't know I was a lesbian. "You've gotta be kidding," one girl teased me, "Everyone knows!"

Often, unravelling the knot that was my own coming out coincided with development of the group...Most of the times that I acted with any reluctance had much more to do with my own process of coming out than with the task at hand. With my computer-keyboard hindsight, it takes only a mirror to measure my gains against my losses. The profit is in the way I see myself. I lost nothing while growing in ways that I'm still discovering. As much as I worked for the sake of justice, for the sake of my students, my colleagues, the school, working for lesbian and gay visibility was directly linked to increases in my own self-esteem.

Sharon's succesor was a young man whose confidence and self-esteem blossomed. Sharon is, as this story indicates, brave and wise beyond her years. Her acts of courage were the seeds of the present Gay/Straight Alliance, and in her two years as leader she inspired others to tend those vineyards. Her twelfth-grade actions were far more convincing than her ninth-grade journal - her life stands as concrete evidence that lesbian and gay heroes do exist. She is living proof that a person's homosexuality does not inhibit one's ability to give support to a friend or vision to a nation.

When I sent an earlier draft of this article for feedback, she responded with a thirteen-page letter of suggestions - delightful and insightful reflections on her understanding of the experience. As always, Sharon's critique was creative, constructive, and candid:

I find it slightly amusing to hear a bunch of mixed-up high school kids, and adults who had no more clue about how to do what we were doing, described in terms like "coalition building" and "context" and "inclusivenes." We played it

48

all by ear, with a lot of hard work and risk. It almost sounds like we knew how the politics of such a group had to worked out. Adult-type politics. As though we planned to model ourselves on something. But we didn't...We didn't consciously work through the politics - at least the students didn't - and for anyone trying to get advice from this article, it sounds like they'd need incredible skills.

Just as Sharon's vision had helped move me to new levels of visibility and strength, her suggestions for revision stand not only as a pleasant reminder of how much fun we all had amid the confusion and chaos of the process, but also as a valuable reminder that our actions were not all precipatated by air-tight philosophical planning.

Time and time again, lines of disagreement ran across the line separating gay and straight. Constantly, the allied effort, however, worked in everyone's best interest. The call for classroom attention to lesbian and gay issues came not only from an unmarried, boots-and-jeans woman with three earrings and a dog, but also from a happily married woman with a station wagon and a tenth-grade son - we were grateful for imput from both women. The reluctance of the lesbian and gay faculty, however, to join the effort may be the strongest reminder of how much remains to be done, of how important it is that some people work for change in the public eye.

Across New England, more than twenty schools with Gay/Straight Alliances of their own have united their efforts. They have gone past *imagining* regional dances, retreats, and conferences by actually organizing and participating in them. Many of the students finding strength and support from their Gay/Straight Alliance testified at public hearings in Massachusetts before the Governor's Commission on Gay and Lesbian Youth. In the spring of 1993, The Gay and Lesbian School Teachers' Network (GLSTN) sponsored The Third Annual GLSTN Conference, "Celebration and Challenge." Students, faculty and administrators from scores of schools participated in a wonderful array of workshops including "Unlearning Internalized Homophobia," "Becoming Visible: Including Gay/Lesbian History in Curriculum," "Talking about Gay and Lesbian Lives in Elementary School Classroom," and "Know Your Rights."

It didn't surprise me to hear that Phillips Academy had been well represented at the conference. My old pals, Kathy, one of the co-founders of GLSTN, Cilla, and Pam all participated in workshops, along with a number of their colleagues. In October, 1992, less than five years from that first informal meeting of a few people in a basement office, Phillips Academy recognized National Coming Out Day with an all-school meeting. Kathy, who has been out on campus for a number of years, spoke at that meeting about being gay. And while so much has already happened that was once beyond my imagination, I also know there's a long way to go. Fortunately, there are Kathys, Cillas, Pams and Sharons out there to inspire others to try.

So if you are, as Sharon would say, "trying to get advice from this article," don't go away thinking you need "incredible skills." I think the best advice I can give, what I believe describes our process, is this: imagine a better world, find others who share your vision, and then build it together. Change won't happen unless you try.

ABOUT THE AUTHOR

Nancy Boutilier ❖ *Teaches in an independent high school in San Francisco. She, along with a number of her colleagues, is out to the entire school community, and wouldn't have it any other way. ACCORDING TO HER CONTOURS, published by Black Sparrow Press, is a collection of her poems and short stories. Her writing appears regularly in THE BAY AREA REPORTER, for which she writes a bi-weekly column called "Dykeotomy," and GIRLJOCK magazine.*

THE BLACK TRIANGLE: In Nazi Germany, lesbians, along with gay men, were put into concentration camps. They were forced to wear the black triangle, while the men wore pink triangles.

oN tHe LIGHteR SIde

IMAGINE THAT

Last spring the local press ran a story titled: **BEING GAY TODAY**. A section with my photo, sitting under a blossoming dogwood tree and reading Jonathan Katz' **GAY AMERICAN HISTORY** was included. A few days later, my former partner of 10 years - and the woman with whom we raised our children - called me to diiscuss the article. "Sue," she said, "Do you remember my Aunt Mary? Well, you're not going to believe this. After she read the article, she called me, shouting from the other end of the phone: 'Imagine that! You   living all those years with **THAT** woman, and not knowing she was a lesbian!'"
                                                    - Sue M.C.

Dee

I always had a confident stride, and held my head high, firmly planting one foot in front of the other, even in third grade (dates back to the '40's). But I'll never forget the teacher who used to say, "Dee, stop that strut! And walk more like a lady." She'd do all kinds of things to get me to change my natural gait - put books on my head and make me take shorter steps... Well, here I am at 57, and - I'm proud to say - I still have that strut!

Dee ❖ *Former proprietor of a thriving dog grooming business, she now resides in Jersey with her two German Shepards.*

51

A HUMAN VISUAL AID?

*...Although I am not a teacher, I regularly go to High School Health
classes to be a "human visual aid" on homosexuality. Here are some
of my observations from a comedian's perspective.*

*...Schools: I don't understand why they don't want homosexuals to teach.
Unfortunately, a large number of today's kids are into drugs, gangs,
wilding and satanic rituals. But heaven forbid! Let's not let the homos teach
them vocabulary...that'll really mess them up!*

*...Actually, having an openly lesbian or gay teacher will not make
children gay. Let's face it, I had straight teachers... it didn't affect me.*

❖❖❖❖❖❖❖❖❖❖❖❖❖❖❖❖❖❖❖❖❖❖❖❖❖❖❖❖❖❖❖❖❖❖❖

*Suzanne Westenhoefer ❖ A truly out lesbian comic, is a summer
regular at THE POST OFFICE, Provincetown, Cape Cod, Massachusetts.
She has hosted myriad fund raisers for the lesbigay community in NYC -
The Palladium, The Lime Light, Fat Cats, Crazy Nanny's and has
performed for NYC and N.J. Lesbian and Gay March rallies. In '91,
Suzanne took her comedy to the SALLY JESSY RAPHAEL SHOW where
she helped in "breaking the lesbian stereotype," and has hosted Gay
Cable Network. Women's events include: Campfest, East Coast Lesbian
Music and Arts Festival, Michigan Women's Music Festival, West Coast
Women's Comedy and Southern Women's Music. A regular at
THE IMPROV, and other clubs (both straight and gay) across the country.
Co-host at THE 1993 LESBIAN, GAY AND BISEXUAL MARCH ON WASHINGTON.*

❖❖❖❖❖❖❖❖❖❖❖❖❖❖❖❖❖❖❖❖❖❖❖❖❖❖❖❖❖❖❖❖❖❖❖

WORKING WITH LESBIAN AND GAY ADOLESCENTS

by Michael Singervalt

As a gay man working in secondary education, one of my dreams was to help lesbian, gay and bisexual adolescents come to terms with their gender orientation. I have long since come to terms with who I am, I knew that I could provide the positive support these young people needed. Adolescents, struggling to define their gender orientation, often do so in isolation, victims of the misinformation society perpetuates about homosexuality. Without proper support, this process can be a long and difficult one.

In high school, I knew there was something different about me, but I wasn't ready to use the label - homosexual. The idea that I might be gay was abhorrent to me, at first. Since I had not met any people that I knew to be lesbian or gay, the only definition I had of homosexuality was what I heard in the media or on the street. Nothing within my elementary or secondary education counteracted these myths. Although I repressed the notion that I was gay, a small part of me must have known the truth. I spent so much time and energy avoiding anything that would have made my gender orientation clear to me. I dated girls, not because I wanted to, but because I was expected to. I avoided any physical contact with other boys, for fear that I might be labeled a "faggott." I knew enough not to talk to anyone about the way I felt. Had someone approached me then, asking if I had some questions about my gender orientation, I would have freaked. As much as I may have been hurting inside, I was just not ready to face this issue head on. The confusion about who I was, and the isolation I felt, led to depression and a suicide attempt in my senior year of high school. I had reached a level of unhappiness no one, not even I, could understand. I'm sure people, especially my parents were concerned, but no one could figure out, "What's the matter with Michael?" I knew that no matter how bad I felt, it was better to suffer in silence than to risk being exposed as a homosexual. Even after a serious attempt at taking my own life (I swallowed a bottle of pain killers I had gotten after I broke my foot in 11th grade), I was forced to deal with the issue of my gender orientation alone. I felt that my family, friends and school were unavailable to me for support.

My story is similar to many young people dealing with these issues. Growing up, lesbian and gay adolescents have one important thing in common with their heterosexual counterparts. Both groups are taught to hate and fear homosexuality. The fact that some of us grow up to become that which we've been taught to hate and fear has a devastating effect on our sense of self. Among school children, the word "gay" is used for anything which is negative or undesirable. Even those of us who eventually "come out" and begin to identify ourselves as lesbian, gay or bisexual, continue to carry around this negative

54

conditioning, unless there's intervention.

Because of this conditioning, I view the coming out process as essentially a traumatic experience. No matter how successful this process is for someone, we worry about possible rejection from loved ones, as well as facing our own homophobia, major contributing factors for the high rate of suicide and drug and/or alcohol abuse for young gays, lesbians and bisexuals.

A 1990 study published by the federal government stated that lesbian and gay youth are two to three times more likely to attempt suicide than their heterosexual counterparts. Most high schools in New Jersey have some sort of suicide prevention programs. How many of them even address the issue of homosexuality? My guess is, few if any.

Also, society is often victim to what Marshall Kirk and Hunter Madsen in their book, AFTER THE BALL, call "The Big Lie" - until the recent media coverage of lesbians and gays in the military - "the nationwide pretense that in America there are really no gays to speak of."

For these reasons, Gay and Lesbian Youth in New Jersey (GALY-NJ) was organized in 1989. It is a support group for adolescents, ages 16-21 who are self-identified as lesbian, gay or bisexual, or who are simply curious about a lesbian or gay way of life. Since many people are still not ready to make this declaration, GALY-NJ provides a space where these people can explore who they are. Co-sponsoring GALY-NJ is the Gay Activist Alliance in Morris County (GAAMC) and Parents and Friends of Lesbians and Gays, Northern New Jersey Chapter (PFLAG).

GALY-NJ was formed to help meet the unique needs of

these adolescents. Its goals are:

1. Provide a non-threatening (e.g., non-sexual, non-alcoholic) environment where lesbian and gay adolescents can begin to understand what it means to be lesbian or gay.

2. To reduce the extreme sense of isolation (e.g., "Am I the only one who feels this way?").

3. To provide the opportunity to experience some of the social events (such as dating) normally unavailable to lesbian and gay adolescents.

4. To help the lesbian or gay adolescent "unlearn" the misconceptions that society perpetuates.

5. To provide positive lesbian and gay adult role models.

6. To provide information and support about critical life issues, such as coming out to parents.

7. To furnish accurate information about AIDS and safer sex practices.

8. To foster a sense of pride in oneself through exposure to positive lesbian and gay history and culture.

9. To help lesbian or gay adolescents to develop the inner resources to enable them to protect themselves better from the homophobic reactions of others.

Since its inception, the organization has had several hundred people come through its doors. Some have been coming since the beginning. Adult volunteers are carefully screened, and no contact is permitted between group members and adult volunteers except for planned group activities.

Starting a group like GALY-NJ presented some interesting problems.   We really had no one to learn from. Most youth groups, including two in New York, are in urban areas. GALY-NJ is located in the suburbs, not easily accessible. Also, after meeting with representatives from the Hetrick-Martin Institute (formerly the Institute for Protection of Lesbian and Gay Youth), and Gay and Lesbian Youth In New York, we found New Jersey youth had different issues.

GALY-NJ is not a therapy group. Its main function is to provide young people with a social outlet and to allow them to interact with each other in a safe and structured place. Heterosexual adolescents have the opportunity to develop appropriate social skills as they grow. They have adults and peers to serve as role models. The media uses straight sex to sell everything from toothpaste to automobiles. Art and music are dedicated to heterosexual love. Lesbian, gay and bisexual adolescents are unable to engage in appropriate social situations because none of them are available to them. Think how your school would react if someone tried to bring a same-sex date to the prom.

By and large, the single most important issue young people bring to GALY-NJ is their families. One way or another, family is discussed at most every meeting. These young people have a lot to lose if their parents find out about them and react badly. More than once, a young person has shown up at our doorstep, suitcase in hand, because their parents kicked them out. Some of this is beginning to change; many youth people now feel the silence and deceit are more harmful. Yet, GALY-NJ neither encourages or discourages a young person from coming out to

his or her family. Each decision has consequences. What
GALY-NJ encourages is for each person to wait until -
- s/he has had time to sort through her/his feelings
- s/he has learned the facts so that questions parents may
have can be answered intelligently
- s/he has considered all the possible consequences
- s/he has a strong network (such as GALY-NJ) in place
to help her/him through that rough period
   Why GALY? Just as a coin has two sides, when one
initially realizes that one is lesbian, gay or bisexual, if a person
is fortunate, s/he soon discovers a whole new world exists for
him or her. Our community is rich in history, culture and
tradition. The world is only now beginning to realize the
enormous contributions our community has made. When we
come out, we can begin to develop an insider's view of our new
world. We can learn a new language (Oh Mary, please!), we get
new holidays (Lesbian and Gay Pride Weekend in June), we
learn that there are alternatives to life other than getting married,
having children (unless we want to).
   Perhaps more importantly, however, by meeting "real"
homosexuals (and not the one dimensional stereotypes we were
taught to believe in), we can begin to change the underlying
beliefs we have of ourselves, perceiving ourselves in more
positive light. Older members of our community have a lot to
offer the younger ones. Those of us who have been able to
make a life for ourselves despite negative social pressure, need
to pass this strength on. History is full of women and men who
have lived their lives successfully under unthinkable oppression.
   If a group like GALY-NJ can have such a tremendous

58

impact on our youth, imagine the kind of impact that schools could have. Remember, for every young person that makes it to GALY, many do not. Support services must be brought to them. Schools and other youth support agencies must first accept the fact that these young people exist. They must then make the commitment to help. Opposition from homophobes or a poor political climate is no excuse. Those of us who work with young people are responsible for their welfare. All of them. Not just the ones who are socially correct.

As educators, we are in a position to make positive change. It doesn't have to happen on a grand scale. Quietly, one young person at a time is enough.

ABOUT THE AUTHOR

Michael Singervalt ❖ *A school psychologist in New Jersey, K-12 since receiving his MA in 1979, Michael's certification extends to New York. A member of the National Education Association, New Jersey Education Association and the National Association of School Psychologists, he has been on the executive board of GALY-NJ since its inception. Speaking engagements include ON THE LINE, a lesbian and gay radio show, school workshops and conventions. He resides in North Jersey with his life-partner, Paul.*

PART II

UNDERSTANDING

Lesbian
And
Gay

Youth

I Think I Might Be A Lesbian... Excerpts from
Campaign to End Homophobia

• What does it mean to be a lesbian?

Lesbians are women-loving-women. We are women who are sexually attracted to other women. We are women who may feel emotionally and spiritually closer to women. We are women who prefer women as our partners.

As lesbians, we are not alone. One out of ten teenagers is lesbian or gay. Many famous women in history were lesbians. Lesbians are teachers, doctors, lawyers, factory workers, police officers, politicians, ministers, movie stars, artists, mothers, nuns, truck drivers, models, novelists. You name it, we do it.

Lesbians are white, Black, Asian, Hispanic, Native American, Jewish, Catholic, Protestant, Buddhist. Lesbians are rich, poor, working class, and middle class. Some lesbians are in heterosexual marriages. Some lesbians are disabled. Lesbians are young women and old women. you name it, we are it.

Lesbians live in the cities and in the country. We are everywhere.

...now what do I do?

• How do I know if I'm a lesbian?

"When I was young I always wanted to grow up and live with my best girlfriend, and that feeling never changed as I got older."
Tammy, age 17

"When we're really young, we have crushes on girls, but then we're supposed to grow out of it. We're supposed to read books about how girl meets boy and boy meets girl. Well, I'd never finish those books."
Terryle, age 16

During adolescence, most young women begin to be aware of sexual feelings and take an interest in dating. Many young women feel physically attracted to men. But many other young women feel physically attracted to other women.

You may notice that you feel turned on by other women. You may feel different from your girlfriends, like you don't fit in sometimes. When your girlfriends are checking out boys, you may find yourself checking out girls. Going out with boys may not interest you. You may find yourself wondering, "Why aren't there any men like these terrific women I keep meeting?"

You may also feel confused or unsure about whether or not you're a lesbian. Many adults will tell us that we're too young to call ourselves gay, or that we're going through a phase, or that we don't know what we're talking about. That's their way of avoiding the fact that some of us are lesbian youth.

You may feel confused because you're attracted to both men and women. That's OK. Some women have relationships with both men and women throughout their lives. Some may later decide to be exclusively lesbian or heterosexual.

Our sexuality develops over time. Don't worry if you aren't sure.

"I think we're very brave to have recognized this in ourselves and to have wanted to come to terms with it."
Natalie, age 18

Yes, you are normal. It's perfectly natural for people to be attracted to members of their own sex. But it's not something that's encouraged in our society. Many people push away these feelings because of prejudice against gay men and lesbians.

Most scientific experts agree that a person's sexual orientation is determined at a very young age, maybe even at birth.

It's normal and healthy to be yourself, whether you're gay or straight. What's really important is that we learn to like ourselves.

• What is it like to be young and lesbian?

"I feel very powerful, special, independent, strong, and courageous."
Natalie, age 18

"It's scary sometimes. I've felt very unsure of myself. But other times I feel wonderful and proud."
Terryle, age 16

There's no "right" way or "wrong" way to be a lesbian. Because of society's stereotypes about lesbians that we've all grown up with, you might think you have to be a certain way if you're a lesbian. But lesbians come in all shapes and sizes, from all occupations, and with all levels of education.

Your sexual orientation is only one part of who you are. You probably have hobbies and interests that are the same as your straight friends.

"Once I accepted myself and my sexuality, I found that I became more involved in life with my friends because I was more comfortable with myself."

Tammi, age 18

"I feel down and depressed a lot because of the homophobia that I'm constantly up against, but then I realize that I have the power to educate other members of my generation."

Tammy, age 17

• Who should I tell?

"You shouldn't feel pressured to tell anyone at all until you are comfortable with the idea of being a lesbian yourself. Be prepared that people's reactions will vary."

Tammi, age 18

"Only tell someone if you feel you have enough support to face what may happen. Try to tell someone if you think you can't deal with these feelings alone anymore. If you think your family might flip out, tell someone who might be more impartial."

Sarah, age 19

"When I told a couple of my friends, I told them I was no different now than I was five minutes before I told them, except that now I wasn't keeping a big secret from them."

Terryle, age 16

Coming out is the process of accepting yourself as a lesbian and figuring out how open you want to be about your sexual orientation.

Unfortunately, not everyone you know will think that being a lesbian is the greatest thing since sliced bread. It's hard to know who can handle the information and give you support. Some friends may accept you. Some may turn away from you or tell other people without your permission. Telling family can be very difficult. Some families are very supportive. But some lesbian and gay youth have been kicked out of their homes when their parents found out.

Maybe there's a guidance counselor or social worker in your school, or in a local youth or counseling agency, that you can trust. It's important to have someone to talk to because it's not normal or healthy for young people to have to keep secret such an important part of their lives.

• What about sex?

"First I would ask myself if I felt ready. Then I would talk to my partner to see if she felt ready. When you decide to have sex, it feels good when you've made the right decision. Only you can know when it is and isn't right for you to have sex."

Tammi, age 18

"Just because you're turned on to someone doesn't mean you're ready to have sex. You have to feel emotionally ready. It's important that the two people talk about what they like and don't like. No one should have to do something they don't want to do. There's no need to rush things. It'll come in time."

Terryle, age 16

• How do we learn to like ourselves?

"It's important that we don't deny our feelings. If we be who we truly want to be in our hearts, we can be surprised at how happy we can be. And we should think a lot about all our positive points, and being a lesbian is very positive."
Rebecca, age 16

"It helps me to interact with people who make me feel happy and good about myself. And I try to do things I feel good about doing."
Sarah, age 19

All people have a right to feel good about themselves. We're all valuable human beings. Developing self-esteem is very important for young people. It's hard for gay and lesbian youth to feel good about ourselves because all around us are people who believe that we're sick, or perverted, or destined to live very unhappy lives.

When we feel like we have to hide who we really are, it can make us feel like hurting ourselves, like through alcohol, drugs, or suicide. We may feel very isolated, fearful, and depressed, especially if we've had no one to talk to about the fact that we're lesbians.

More and more, we, as young lesbians, are learning to like who we are. It helps to read good books about lesbians — books that have accurate information in them and that are written about lesbians who are leading very fulfilling lives. It also helps to meet other lesbians because then we find out that lesbians are as diverse as any other group of people and that we've been told a lot of lies by our society.

It can help to say to yourself every day, "I'm a lesbian and I'm OK." And try to find someone to talk to who also believes that lesbians are OK. Remember: it's normal and natural to be a lesbian, just like it's normal and natural for some people to be heterosexual.

• How can I meet other lesbians?

"There are many lesbians around you, but you don't know they're lesbians, just as they don't know that you're a lesbian. Don't lose hope. You'll eventually meet some."
Sarah, age 19

- Make contact with local feminist organizations like the National Organization for Women (NOW).
- Many colleges and universities have campus gay, lesbian, and feminist organizations.
- Check your phone book for a local hotline and ask for the gay and lesbian organizations in your area. There might even be a gay/lesbian youth group in your area.
- Look for a gay/lesbian or feminist newspaper in your area. Check local bookstores, health food stores, and gay bars for copies.

• Do I have to worry about AIDS?

All of us should know about HIV, the virus believed to be the cause of AIDS — how it's transmitted and how we can prevent ourselves from becoming infected. You and your partner should discuss your risk factors for HIV infection and decide what, if any, safer sex methods you should use.

I think I might be gay . . . *excerpts from*

Campaign to End Homophobia

• What does it mean to be gay?

Men who call themselves gay are sexually attracted to and fall in love with other men. Their sexual feelings toward men are normal and natural for them. These feelings emerge when they are boys and the feelings continue into adulthood. Although some gay men may also be attracted to women, they usually say that their feelings for men are stronger and more important to them.

We know that about one out of ten people in the world is gay or lesbian (lesbians are women who are attracted to other women). This means that in any large group of people, there are usually several gay people present. However, you cannot tell if someone is gay or not unless he or she wants you to know. Gay people blend right in with other people. But they often <u>feel</u> different from other people.

Gay teenagers may not be able to specify just why they feel different. All of the guys they know seem to be attracted to girls, so they don't know where they fit in. And, they may not feel comfortable talking with an adult about their feelings.

. . .now what do I do?

65

• How do I know if I'm gay?

"I don't remember exactly when I first knew that I was gay, but I do remember that the thought of sex with men always excited me."

Alan, age 19

"I never had any real attraction towards women, but I really knew that I was gay when puberty began. I felt an attraction toward the other boys and I was curious to find out what they were like."

James, 17

"One day I was flipping through a magazine, there was a cute guy, and bam! I knew."

Antonio, age 16

You may not know what to call your sexual feelings. You don't have to rush and decide how to label yourself right now. Our sexual identities develop over time. Most adolescent boys are intensely sexual during the years around puberty (usually between 11 and 15 years old), when their bodies start changing and their hormones are flowing in new ways. Your sexual feelings may be so strong that they are not directed toward particular persons or situations, but seem to emerge without cause. As you get older you will figure out who you are really attracted to.

66

Boys with truly gay feelings find that, over time, their attractions to boys and men get more and more clearly focused. You may find yourself falling in love with your classmates or maybe developing a crush on a particular adult man. You may find these experiences pleasurable, troubling, or a mix of the two. By age 16 or 17 many gay kids start thinking about what to call themselves, while others prefer to wait.

If you think you might be gay, ask yourself:

- When I dream or fantasize sexually, is it about boys or girls?

- Have I ever had a crush or been in love with a boy or a man?

- Do I feel different than other guys?

- Are my feelings for boys and men true and clear?

If you cannot answer these questions now, don't worry. You will be more sure in time. You and only you know how to label yourself correctly.

• Learning to like yourself

"I had to reject a lot of negative heterosexual and religious programming that made me feel lousy about myself as a gay person. I began to like myself by meeting other gay people and going to a gay support group. After that I was content with myself."

Bill, age 18

"My aunt is a lesbian, and she made it clear to me , before I even knew I was gay, that being gay was OK."

Antonio, age 16

"I accepted the facts, which means that I don't deny being gay and I don't pretend to be someone I'm not."

Alan, 19

It's not easy to discover that you are gay. Our society makes it very clear what it thinks of gay people. We all hear the terrible jokes, the hurtful stereotypes and the wrong ideas that circulate about gay people. People tend to hate or fear what they don't understand.Some people hate gay lesbians and gay men. Many people are uncomfortable being around lesbians and gay men.

It's no wonder that you might choose to hide your gay feelings from others. You might even be tempted to hide them from yourself.

You may wonder if you are normal. Perhaps you worry about people finding out about you. Maybe you avoid other kids who might be gay because of what people will think. Working this hard to conceal your thoughts and feelings is called being in the closet. It is a painful and lonely place to be, even if you stay there in order to survive.

It takes a lot of energy to deny your feelings, and it can be costly. You may have tried using alcohol or other drugs to numb yourself against these thoughts. You may have considered suicide. If so, please consult the phone-book for the Samaritans or another hotline. There are alternatives to denying your very valuable feelings. Check out the resources listed on the back of this brochure.

• Who should I tell?

"I only tell other people that I'm gay if I've known them for a long time and if they are accepting and tolerant. I think it's important that they know about this special part of me."
Bill, age 18

"I tell people that I'm gay if I know that they won't reject me, will accept me for what I am, and won't try to 'straighten' me out. I test them, I suppose, then I judge if I want to risk telling them."

John, age 17

More and more gay kids are learning to feel better about themselves. As you start to listen to your deepest feelings and learn more about what it means to be gay you will begin to be comfortable with your sexuality. This is the process called coming out.

• What about AIDS?

All sexually active people need to be aware of AIDS as well as other sexually transmitted diseases. Being gay does not give you AIDS, but certain sexual practices and certain drug use behaviors can put you at risk for catching the virus that causes AIDS. AIDS is incurable, but is preventable.

67

What can you do? Your best friend has just told you, "I'm gay."

Stop Telling Queer Jokes

*Because they're based on lies and you may be hurting someone you care about.
*Put downs say more about you, and mean you don't understand.

Find An Understanding Adult

-Because realizing you're gay can be confusion and lonely- we all need support.
*Remember, not everyone will be helpful...choose carefully.

Don't Go Away

*Because your friend is in need of someone to lean on.
*Trusting is a sign of friendship.

DID YOU KNOW THAT...

• Ten percent of all the people you know are, or will be discovering that they are, gay or lesbian.

• People seldom expect to make such a discovery. When they do, they are often surprised and sometimes uncomfortable with the feelings. They may also fear being ridiculed or hurt.

• Fear makes people want to hide. Hiding is a heavy burden. Trusting you is the first step in relieving that burden.

• If you are gay/lesbian or have a friend who is, it's not the end of the world. Countless others have made this same discovery and are leading meaningful, happy lives.

IF YOU WANT MORE INFORMATION

For accurate information, a safe, confidential place to call is:
Gay and Lesbian Community Action Council
HELPLINE 822-8661

or after hours call YES at 379-6363
or contact someone here at

68

DID YOU KNOW THAT –

- Ten percent of all the people you know are, or will be
discovering that they are gay or lesbian.
- People seldom expect to make such a discovery. When
they do, they are often surprised and sometimes
uncomfortable with the feelings. They may also fear being
ridiculed or hurt.
- Fear makes people want to hide. Hiding is a heavy burden.
Trusting you is the first step in relieving that burden.
- If you are gay/lesbian or have a friend who is, it's not the
end of the world. Countless others have made this same
discovery and are leading meaningful, happy lives.
- Most of us don't know much about what it means to be gay
or lesbian. In fact both you and your friend may have many
of the same questions. Helping find accurate information is
one way of being a friend.
- We all have the same need for love and friendship. It's not
who you love that is so important. It's that you love and are
a friend.

If you want more information please call (612) 224-3371. To
purchase the WINGSPAN POSTER send $5.00 to St. Paul-
Reformation Lutheran Church, Attn: Leo Treadway, 100 North
Oxford Street, Saint Paul, Minnesota 55104

THE TRIANGULAR TUBE OF PINK LIPSTICK *by Gail Watnick*

I lay in bed with my eyes closed. I visualize the make-up sitting on my dresser, and my mother lying in her bed visualizing the make-up and wishing it were on my face instead of the dresser. I open my eyes and see the square blue eyeshadow box and the triangular tube of pink lipstick. My parents! They buy me a pink lipstick and think it will hide my sexual feelings toward other women if I put it on my lips.

I lay on my back glancing occasionally at the ceiling and the make-up. I really thought it would make my life easier if I told them how I was feeling. So instead of hiding my true self, I announced that I thought I might be a lesbian. I was grappling with this issue for four years and was wondering what my future would be like as a homosexual. What is life like when you are thirty, or forty? And what will my neighbors think? I hope they are not as hostile as my parents are; if so, I had better continue suppressing my feelings, I thought.

The decision to be open and honest with my parents followed much soul searching. I no longer wanted to act or wear a mask and I believed they could offer me some support. Unhappily, however, they were not understanding at all, making me feel worthless and as if all of my prior achievements meant nothing.

I lay in bed staring at the make-up. Putting it on would make my distraught mother happy. To them, it would mean I was no longer gay - as simple as that. They tried their hardest to change me. They felt that letting my hair grow would somehow change my feelings and no longer make me feel sexually attracted to women. Wearing fancy shoes would change that too. Well, the only things that wearing fancy shoes would change was getting me blisters.

Then they tried some really crazy things (I was not that calm myself). They went out and bought me a beautiful flower print bedcover with matching sheets. They would have looked wonderful on someone else's bed but not on mine. It just was not me to have flowered sheets. My mother ripped off my favorite red, yellow, blue, and green striped sheets and put these on. In turn, I ripped off the flowered sheets and replaced it with my favorite stripes. We took turns and created this pointless action two more times. We were struggling to fit me in, just as we were trying to fit the bed with the "right" pattern. My mother's pattern consisted of marriage and kids.

I lay on my flowered sheets looking at the make-up thinking, "I wonder if I am going to be a lesbian all of my life and if so, will my parents every accept me?"

Yesterday, my father refused to talk to me. Mother said he felt that he gave me so much love and opportunity, and he feels like I let him down.

She then insisted that the children I could have were going to be fabulous and that the world would be a lesser place without them. How could I argue with that! When it came right down to it, however, they admitted they did not want the neighbors discriminating against me - and them.

I lay in bed thinking about Robert Frost's poem, "The Road Not Taken". Reciting the last two lines, "I took the road less traveled by,/And that has made all the difference," I realized the confrontation with my family has changed my view of the poem. I used to think the difference referred to individuality and following one's own heart; that in itself would create positive effects.

I lay in bed. I think about the unrealistic options my family created for me - women or men, pink lipstick or not.

ABOUT THE AUTHOR

Gail Watnick ❖ *Gail was an education major at Yale when she submitted TRIANGULAR TUBE... Since then, her parents have happily come to understand and accept their daughter. She now shares an apartment in Connecticut and enjoys the outdoors with her lover.*

Jayson™   1990 J.A. KRELL
Distributed by TDF

Jeffrey A. Krell ❖ *Jeffrey works for a Manhattan-based market research firm. He graduated summa cum laude and Phi Beta Kappa from the University of Pennsylvania with a B.A. in communications and German in 1982. After four years with Philadelphia advertising agencies, he was offered a full scholarship to persue MBA studies at Emory University. He interned at the Länderbank in Vienna during the summer of 1987, and received his MBA in marketing and finance in 1988.*

In his "spare time" Jeffrey syndicates a cartoon strip called "Jayson" to a dozen gay-oriented publications. "Jayson" debuted in the PHILADELPHIA GAY NEWS (PGN) in 1983 and soon became a staple in GAY COMIX , THE NEW JERSEY NETWORK MAGAZINE, and MEATMAN. "Jayson" has also graced NAL's GAY COMICS anthology and STRIP AIDS USA.

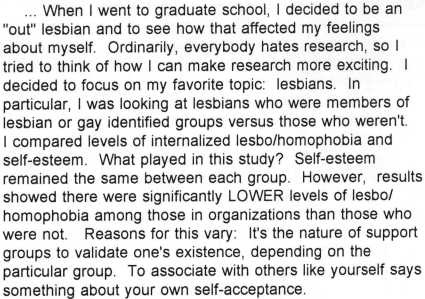

FINDING OTHERS LIKE YOURSELF IS EMPOWERING

interview with Paula Schorr, MSW

... When I went to graduate school, I decided to be an "out" lesbian and to see how that affected my feelings about myself. Ordinarily, everybody hates research, so I tried to think of how I can make research more exciting. I decided to focus on my favorite topic: lesbians. In particular, I was looking at lesbians who were members of lesbian or gay identified groups versus those who weren't. I compared levels of internalized lesbo/homophobia and self-esteem. What played in this study? Self-esteem remained the same between each group. However, results showed there were significantly LOWER levels of lesbo/homophobia among those in organizations than those who were not. Reasons for this vary: It's the nature of support groups to validate one's existence, depending on the particular group. To associate with others like yourself says something about your own self-acceptance.

Paula Schorr, MSW, completed her degree at Rutgers University. A member of a band, FERTILE CRESCENT.

HOLDING MY HEAD UP ONCE MORE

Tamika, 17

After coming out to my best friend two years ago in high school, she betrayed my trust by telling everyone. Since that day, I have lived two years of hell, barely hanging in there 'til graduation last June. Whether in the corridor or lunchroom, classmates would point and call me names. I'd get punched in the face, pinched, or pushed. I used to excel in sports, yet I almost failed, refusing to change or play. In the gym locker room, girls would call me names, making a big fuss about changing in front of a "lezzie". Because of this, I refused to make eye contact with anyone, developing a habit of looking down all the time. Through sheer lesbian resilience, I survived. But life should be more than mere survival. (Even graduation, usually a jubilant occasion, was painstakingly avoided).

Eventually, I was lucky to have discovered a lesbian organization where I can speak with others like me. I am beginning to play sports again and recapture the self-assurance and confidence that I used to get from athletics. And, I have become friends with the women on my softball team. Matter of fact, on the field, camaraderie, skill and strength in all women are respected, not derided. I am beginning to feel a sense of pride in learning my lesbian heritage. I am holding my head up high once more. **- Tamika**, a pseudonym - she still resides with her parents and fears repercussion.

76

A LESBIAN IN SPECIAL EDUCATION

by Andrea Weiss

Self-portrait by Andrea Weiss

I came out when I was 16, which when I was in high school. It was a boarding school for people with special needs. Mine was to take a much needed break from my home-town school. I was having a lot of problems there, all of which related to my learning disability. Every-thing came to a head when I was 16. My family agreed that it was better that I go away to finish up.

It was soon after I arrived that I noticed I spent more time thinking, dreaming and trying to spend just as much time hanging out with girls as I was with the guys. This wasn't easy. To begin with, there weren't a lot of girls, and like most other places at the time - 1979 - homosexuality couldn't even be mentioned, much less acted upon. The counselors there throught it was "inappropriate". Some of the therapists, though, were OK and my second one (the first therapist moved to New England to work) was sympathetic. As far as lesbian or gay groups go, there was nothing! I was stuck.

When I finally realized that I was gay, it honestly came as no surprise to me. I didn't feel a lot of pain and anguish over it. In fact not a lot at all as it really was something I decided must be so after adding all the evidence. If anything, I felt a lot of confusion; while my feelings about women were OK, I still felt I should try to date guys. It took me a long time to get fully out of that mindset. In other words, I started out bi and slowly gravitated towards women.

Well, that situation didn't work out too well. None of the relationships with men lasted because of disinterest from me. The one that did evolve was more of a friendship with a guy named Peter. He was understanding and perceptive. Eventually, this translated into an open relationship. At the same time, I also found that I wanted to explore my sexuality with other women. This made friendships with women impossible; I would always chase them away by coming on to them. That sounds like a contradiction, I know, but it makes sense if you consider that there were no role models around; I didn't know how to respond to women, nor they to me. When you consider that I had no role models, except for the guys, and the love songs on the radio - I listened to heavy metal and hard rock - everybody knows how sexist these were.

Just prior to graduation I finally had something of a relationship with a woman. We met at a special program which was designed for people with learning disabilities. It prepared us to get jobs, find an apartment and maintain a budget. Her name was Alex (pseudonym) and she was tall, thin and very pretty. We were more friends than lovers, nor did we acknowledge that it was anything, hardly sharing more than a backrub. But the counselors saw it differently and did everything they could to keep us apart, even to the point of physically seperating us. It ended when I left; I never saw her again.

78

Things were better at the next place I went, with the exception of one homophobic person, and everybody regarded him as a "jerk" so it was easy to ignore him. At first, I was a bit reluctant to be open. I wanted to fit in OK. But when I saw everyone was cool about it, I felt I could be more honest about myself. In fact - people are usually more understanding than we give them credit for - it got to the point that one of my friends verbally jumped on a new person making an offensive and homophobic remark to me.

About that time (I was now 18), I began attending a school in Philadelphia. Location helped me a lot, since that city has a nicely developed lesbian and gay community, making frequent trips to GIOVANNI'S BOOKSTORE, and becoming familiar with the lesbian/gay owned shops, diners and clubs. I became acquainted with the PHILADELPHIA GAY NEWS (PGN) and saw my first lesbian film, LEANNA. No groups though. I was prevented from staying evenings - there was a strike going on.

One of the newspapers had a "Personal Section" to which I used to connect with others; it led to my first "real relationship" with a woman. But that was short lived as she couldn't do anything sexual without a man present. I went along with that for awhile, but found it was too much for me. I still did the personals, however. After one too many great first dates (after which I never saw the person again), I stopped answering them.

❖ ❖

ABOUT THE AUTHOR

Andrea Weiss ❖ *Currently majoring in photography, Andrea likes music, art, reading and traveling. She is working on a book and enjoys bike riding.*

❖ ❖

SUE ZAMPA - A Profile
photos by Andrea Weiss

80

"LOTS OF ADVANTAGES FOR A WOMAN COMING OUT..."

interview with Sue Zampa

"I came out to myself in high school aware that something was going on but I continued dating boys. I borrowed every book in the library, too, about the subject. There wasn't much. Only dry, psychological stuff, very negative, very disappointing. Yet, I knew lesbians and gays were all around me, especially since I was in the Drum Corps in that Connecticut town."

..."At the age of 15 or 16, I fell madly and wildly in love with a classmate named Joan V...She was a lesbian and we hung out with this 'artsy' group. She always sat behind me in class - you see, the students were alphabetically arranged and we were the only two letters after "P". This drove me crazy! I was passionate for her, watching her every move. Eventually I got up the nerve to go over to her house and drink tea with her."

..."Actually, I dated boys, and even lived with one guy when I began college at 19. Until I learned about gay bars. It was through a new friend. She took me to a gay bar and my whole life changed. Not that the establishment itself was anything special - it had three floors, the women were in the basement. But this was the first opportunity I had to be myself. The next day, I confronted the guy; he seemed to understand. I had selected a man who had very caring, feminine ways, androgynous.

"New Haven was a great place to live, filled with bookstores, lively dances - called Moon Dances - the Women's Center and a lesbian coffeehouse - lots of advantages for a woman coming out! Social and cultural opportunities abounded! Also reading was very instrumental. I devoured books like Virginia Woolf's ORLANDO, and Tennessee Williams plays because these gifted writers were rumoured to be of our sexual orientation. I listened to the musical notes of Meg Christian's ODE TO A

GYM TEACHER (yes, we still have crushes on our female gym teachers) a thousand times, cherishing each lyric. I am still amazed at variety of materials available today through lesbian/gay bookstores and catalogues, and look forward to a time when I can find materials at any library or store.

Today, in their effort to service a broader base (and of course in recognition of the huge lesbian and gay green power), merchants regularly stock records by chanteuse k.d. lang and the late Freddie Mercury. And "around the corner" video shops display the highly popular DESERT HEARTS.

Yes, it's a great decade to be coming out!

"Before I complete this interview, one area that particularly concerns me is women and the medical profession. I hope to see more studies in print on the subject. It's my belief that women - especially lesbians - don't go to doctors. Why? In addition to the inherent sexism the media has recently brought to light, but we always knew, doctors always ask about birth control. When they ask that question, you only have two choices: to give inaccurate information (celibacy?), or to say you are a lesbian. But if you do that, get ready for a heavy discussion - sometimes I don't want to go over it again and again - discomfort or discrimination. Also, consider this: most of the issues they cover deal with men, not women. Yet every lesbian I know has lost two or three friends to breast or ovarian cancer because they were misdiagnosed or not diagnosed in time. Lesbians do not get adequate medical treatment..."

❖❖❖❖❖❖❖❖❖❖❖❖❖❖❖❖❖❖❖❖❖❖❖❖❖❖❖❖❖❖❖❖❖❖❖

Sue Zampa ❖ *District manager of a large chain retail store. Former producer/host of a Connecticut -based lesbian and gay radio show, Sue co-founded a thriving lesbian rap group. She is currently a member of the QUILT NAMES PROJECT and resides at the beautiful Jersey Shore with her partner of four years, where she enjoys delicious gourmet cooking.*

❖❖❖❖❖❖❖❖❖❖❖❖❖❖❖❖❖❖❖❖❖❖❖❖❖❖❖❖❖❖❖❖❖❖❖

82

I once talked to a gay man who attended schools in Philadelphia. He said when he was in school, he was beaten up mercilessly during the course of the day - in the lockers, hallways, playground. In order to avert additional beatings, he virtually memorized every bus route in the city to get home, taking him three hours each night. Let's make school safe for ALL youth. ▪ Radio statement by John Gish, whose civil rights work dates back to the 70's . Former trustee of the ACLU, NJ, and PR legislative co-chair for the NJ Lesbian and Gay Coalition, Gish was the first NJ educator to contest discrimination against gays in court.

TAKE THE CHALLENGE

written by an anonymous ESL teacher, Newark, NJ

At the age of 5l, the ravages of "Closetitis" had caught up with me: I had a nervous breakdown. It happened as a result of cumulative effects; 30 years of trying to lead a life of compromise in the hetereosexual community - which really doesn't work. Prior to the breakdown, I enjoyed a successful life as educator, receiving a Bachelor's Degree from NYU, two Master's degrees and earned recognition in Phi Beta Kappa. I was a professor of French, Spanish and English. In spite of my outstanding abilities, and my friendly personality, at that time, hints of gayness colored everyone's actions towards me. But the world is swiftly changing, for the better. Lesbians, gay men and bisexuals are carrying on with their lives, with pride. Others are watching them as examples of pathfinders, especially in role-breaker occupations such as women in sports and men in grammar school education. They are providing the role models for contemporary lesbian and gay youth. And it's up the educational community to take up the challenge, smash the strict gender roles, and treat each and every student as the special individuals they are. Society doesn't realize the damage caused by unkindness. Believe me. I lived through it.

83

BitterSweet

by Charles Haver

SISSIES!

HEY, BUZZ! WOULD YOU MIND CLARIFYING FOR US WHAT CONSTITUTES A SISSY?

CERTAINLY! A SISSY IS A GUY WHO LIKES PINK! SISSIES LIKE TO PLAY DRESS-UP WITH THEIR MOTHERS CLOTHES! SISSIES LIKE TO COOK! SISSIES SLEEP WITH TEDDY BEARS!

SISSIES SAY "BLESS YOU" WHEN SOMEBODY SNEEZES! SISSIES TAKE BATHS—REAL MEN ALWAYS TAKE SHOWERS! SISSIES LIKE TO PLAY WITH GIRLS! THEY LIKE TO PLAY HOUSE, HOPSCOTCH AND JACKS! SISSIES LIKE TO JUMP ROPE AND PLAY WITH DOLLS! SISSIES DON'T LIKE TO PLAY BALL! SISSIES STOP TO SMELL THE FLOWERS— REAL MEN JUST WALK ON 'EM!

SISSIES SIT ON THE TOILET TO PEE! SISSIES LOOK AT THEIR FINGERNAILS FROM THE BACK OF THEIR HAND! SISSIES CRY! AND WHAT'S WORSE, THEY GO CRYING TO THEIR MOMMIES WHEN THEY GET BEAT UP! SISSIES SKIP! SISSIES GIGGLE! SISSIES CLUTCH THEIR BOOKS IN FRONT OF THEMSELVES WITH BOTH HANDS! SISSIES BLUSH! SISSIES HAVE LIMP WRISTS! AND SISSIES WIGGLE THEIR BUTTS WHEN THEY WALK!

WOW! THAT'S QUITE A COMPREHENSIVE LIST! WHAT DO WE DO NOW, REGINALD?

DON'T MOVE!

Ches ©1990
IN OTHER WORDS... BE MISERABLE!

BitterSweet

by Charles Haver

85

BitterSweet

by Charles Haver

DEAR DIARY, TODAY I WENT SHOPPING WITH MOMMY AND DADDY...

THERE I WAS IN THE TOY DEPT. OF MURFREE'S DEPT. STORE, ADMIRING THE "ARMY JOE" DOLLS, WHEN I SAW IN THE CORNER OF MY EYE THE MOST BEAUTIFUL DOLL I'VE EVER SEEN!

SHE WAS IN THE "GIRLS" SECTION OF THE TOY DEPT. I MOVED CLOSER TO GET A BETTER LOOK. I WAS AFRAID SOMEONE MIGHT SEE ME, BUT I COULDN'T HELP MYSELF!

SHE STOOD IN A CARDBOARD BOX WITH CLEAR PLASTIC OVER IT. SHE WAS WEARING A LONG, SHINY, PINK DRESS WITH MATCHING ELBOW-LENGTH GLOVES & HIGH-HEELED SHOES. SHE HAD A JEWELED CROWN ON HER HEAD...

BitterSweet

by Charles Haver

I WANTED SO BADLY TO TAKE HER OUT OF THAT BOX & BRING HER HOME WITH ME. IT WOULD HAVE BEEN NEAT TO TAKE HER HOME WITH ONE OF THE "ARMY JOE" DOLLS & HAVE THEM BOTH TO PLAY WITH.

I WAS AFRAID THE OTHER CHILDREN WERE BEGINNING TO NOTICE ME. I PRETENDED I WAS LOOKING AT THE OTHER TOYS. THEN I HEARD DADDY CALL ME. HE HAD A STRANGE LOOK ON HIS FACE AND SHOPPING BAGS IN HIS HANDS. I NOTICED A FOOTBALL IN ONE OF THEM.

TIMMY! LET'S GO!

I'LL TRY TO LOOK SURPRISED WHEN I UNWRAP MY FOOTBALL TOMORROW. MERRY CHRISTMAS! GOOD NIGHT!

©1989 Chas.

87

bitterSweet *by Charles Haver*

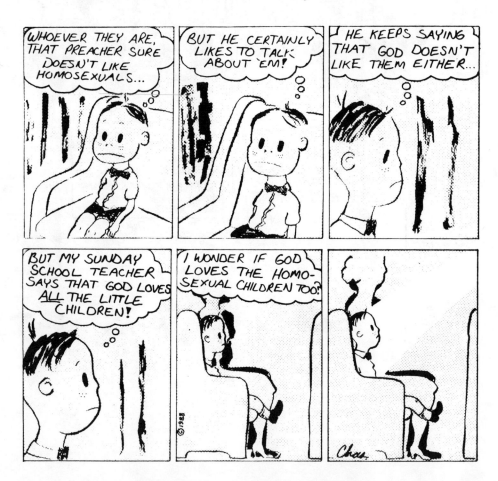

BitterSweet

by Charles Haver

ABOUT THE CARTOONIST

Charles Haver *was the youngest of five children. His father was a minister for the Church of Christ for several years until they became Universalists. They are members of PFLAG (Parents and Friends of Lesbians and Gays). Charles attended Georgia State University in Atlanta, where he still resides with his lover Franklin and two cats, Duncan and Magic. He started drawing BITTERSWEET in 1988 for SOUTHERN VOICE. In the strip, he tries to portray some of the feelings and experiences that lesbian and gay people have as children. He says, "I hope that my cartoon may somehow help gay men and lesbians and heterosexuals get in touch with how homophobia hurts children." BITTERSWEET has appeared in THE WASHINGTON BLADE, DARE (Tenn), MOM, GUESS WHAT (Ca), OUT (New Mexico), PERSPECTIVE (Alaska), EQUAL TIME (Minn) and PGN (Pa).*

HAVING A 'MA'
AS WELL AS A 'MOTHER'

"Same-sex parents often face an extra coming out - and extra stress. At some point in dealing with the school workers and teachers of their children, they must explain the nature of their households. One lesbian couple told us they were concerned that their boy's teacher would become hostile to him when learning he had a 'ma' as well as a 'mother'. It behooves teachers to make it clear to parents and their children, from the beginning, that there are all kinds of families, and that these families are welcome in their school."

- **Demian, Co-Director,**
PARTNERS TASK FORCE FOR GAY AND LESBIAN COUPLES Box 9685, Seattle, WA 98109

THE MANLY KISS

by James Markides

I must admit, when I stepped into that makeshift ring yesterday, I wasn't prepared to fight. But the bell ding-donged, whether I was ready or not, and my opponent hit me in the head. It throbbed and I prayed.

The other boy was Andrew Axman. He is short for a twelve year-old but stronger than most kids on my block. His arms prove it: whenever he flexes his arms for us wide-eyed wimps, his muscles look like tennis balls. Thus, my throbbing head.

Then, with those squinting eyes, his yellow teeth clenched, and those tennis ball arms strategically set, Andrew shot his right arm, and his strongest, into my stomach. I fell onto my knees and wrapped my arms around my waist.

My stomach is the weakest point of my body: one punch into it means certain death (and I thought for sure I was going to die).

I gasped for life.

Then there were the onlookers: other young kids, who came to see Andrew smash me into millions of pieces, commanded me to stand up and fight like a man. Like a man! Can you believe it? I'm only twelve, for frig sake. (Mom told me that an intelligent young boy shouldn't be saying that "f" word, so whenever I wanted to say it, I should just say, "frig." But I don't want to talk about Mom right now). The crowd hollored that they hadn't spent fifty cents just to watch a two minute sock-it-to-him match. They were there to see blood.

91

And Andrew was the most bloodthirsty of them all. He shouted at me to get up so that he could rip off my head, (he could probably do it, too). I tried to get up, but the grass, the trees, the houses, and those ugly kids started to spin. I was going to faint.

But I heard his voice. Zachary Manly, my best friend in the whole wide world, was screaming at me.

"You can do it," he said. I stared into his eyes, they're blue, and I thought, save me Zachary, save me.

Zachary jumped into the ring, like a bird shielding its young, and wrapped his arms around me. He was so warm. The boys and girls laughed and hissed. Zachary, cover my ears, I thought. But Zachary spoke into them, softly, and told me to get up. I couldn't. I felt glued to the grass, or, at least wished I were.

"Get up," he pleaded.

I wanted desperately to tell Zachary that the only reason I had fought was for him. But Zachary would not understand that (and I don't think I do), not at his age anyway. So I got up, cursed my best friend in the whole wide world, and collapsed into my opponent's tennis ball arms.

When I awoke, I was lying far outside that makeshift ring. A thick fog had formed, and the kids were huddled even closer to the ring. I should have crawled away, but instead I crawled closer to watch the action.

Zachary was on top of Andrew. Go Zach go, I whispered. He pulled his right arm back, unafraid, and punched Andrew's face. He punched it again and again until Andrew's blood splashed the grass beneath him. (I was disgusted and delighted from this, I'm ashamed to say). The match was over and I guess

92

you could say their fifty cents was well spent.

Then, I remember, a few boys and girls walking past me and calling me names like "mighty mouse" and "the wimpy whimper." I'm lucky, I didn't start crying. I can imagine what they would have called me if I did.

Everyone left the yard except for Zachary and Maia. The others accompanied a bloody bandaged Andrew through the dense fog. They were going to the next fight Andrew had planned the night before. (Fights are big nowadays).

Maia is my second best friend in the whole wide world (and a beautiful one at that). She has eyes like almonds and lips like cherries. Maia has brains too: she talks incessantly about the stars, especially the constellation Orion.

Zachary and Maia came towards me, her left hand in his. I wanted to barf: I had been holding her hand the night before last. I'll admit, my hand was slippery wet with perspiration. But whose hand isn't at my age? She had betrayed me. But why? I am an inquisitive twelve year-old who needs answers. I asked myself: Is it because Zachary has prettier eyes or whiter teeth than me? Is it because he is taller than me? (I hear from my sisters that women prefer taller men. Well, that might be true, but at my age I still have lots of time to grow). Is it his brain? Surely, it isn't his brain. (I am not the only one who flunked grade five).

"Hey, you OK?" Maia asked me with surprising sympathy.
"I dunno."
"Your stomach sore?" she asked, swinging Zachary's hand.
"Your head sore?"
"Her kindness killed me. I glanced at Zachary, whose head was drooped, and said sincerely: "My head always hurts when I

see you two."

Their hands stopped swinging and separated. Zachary turned to go. I jumped up, grabbed his left shoulder, and turned him towards me. I stared into those pretty blue eyes and tightened my grip, wishing I could hold him there longer than my words had lasted.

"Thanks Zach. You didn't have to, (boy, was I lying) but thanks anyway. I wish I were you. Man, you really zonked Andrew. Guess you're goin' to fight him again, eh Manly?"

"I don't like that kinda fightin', and besides, you were gettin' nailed in there. Anyway, gotta split, I'm cold."

I must admit, he was shivering a lot, so I let him walk away. The fog ate him in seconds.

Well, then it was just Maia and me. Oh boy, was I nervous! She stood silent, smiling, as if I was about to ask her the will-you-be-my-girlfriend question.

"Maia, why did Zach split?"

"Because of you," she answered and stepped closer to me.

My whole world was spinning again, and I felt movement between my legs. I placed my hands in front of them, embarrassed.

"Do you like me," she asked.

"I dunno."

"I mean, do you think I'm pretty like Zach does?"

"I'm not Zach."

"Why don't you kiss me? Zachary does."

"I'm not Zach." I looked down into the grass.

"'Cause if you want to kiss me, you can you know. It's alright."

I began to turn my thoughts to Zachary. What would he do now? Well, he would have kissed her and I hate him for it: kissing girls is easy for him. His legs never go weak; his stomach never feels funny; his thoughts never confused.

"C'mon, give me a kiss. Like Zach does. Give me a manly kiss."

When she said these words, I pushed her aside and ran away into the fog. It ate me in seconds. That evening I lay in Zachary's bed. He had asked me to sleep over and at first I hesitated - remembering Maia's hand in his made it difficult to say yes. But I couldn't say no to him. (In fact, I rarely say no). Sleeping at each other's house is one of the rules of our friendship (bed buddies forever, as Zachary calls us).

We lay in his bed, a foot apart from one another, making sure that no parts of our bodies were touching until we were asleep. That is another rule. It probably sounds silly, I know. But I didn't make it.

I stared up at the window in the middle of Zachary's ceiling. The fog had cleared so I watched the stars, hoping to discuss them with Maia. I found Orion and knew this would impress her. Then, I closed my eyes to shut out the window and its light. His window scares me: I always expect a bug-eyed monster or axe-wielding madman to come bursting through it. But last night, and like other nights, I was comforted as always with Zachary by my side.

"Did you kiss Maia today after the fight?" he asked.

I turned away and stared at the wall in front of me. Did he have to ask me that, I thought.

"No," I said with embarrassment.

"Why not?" he continued.

"'Cause I was mad."

"At what?" Zachary asked cautiously.

"At the two of you," I answered, turning back to face him.

"What for? Maia and I were just holdin' hands. Anyway, you know she likes me."

"But she likes me too, you idiot!" I shouted.

"Well then you should have smacked her a big juicy one," he said as if his answer was the most obvious thing to do.

However, nothing seemed obvious to me at that point. I was utterly confused: it was like the same feeling I got once when I came to a crossroads while riding through the woods. I was riding for hours, so fast Mom would have died if she found out, not worried about where I was going or when I had to be home. But when it got dark, and I was going home, I was suddenly lost and confused when I saw a fork in the road. I was sure it wasn't there before. I asked myself, worried: which way do I go?

"Zach, I've kissed her before. Right on the lips. Bull's-eye!" I said as proud as I could.

"Did you like it big boy?"

Well, I couldn't let him say that and get away with it. So, I jumped on top of him, held his arms above his head, and tickled his stomach. He laughed until he hurt, and I didn't stop until I knew he was hurting. If I couldn't beat him to death, I would make him laugh to death. (And that works every time. Zachary lies there as still as a mummy until I speak).

"Hey Manly, wake up," I said pushing him off the bed.

He stood up and imitated a soldier - legs together, back

straight, and left hand saluting. I have to admit he looked grand. (I love that word). And not only that, Zachary looked much older. In my eyes, my thirteen year-old best friend in the whole wide world (and I'm glad he's mine) was a young man. Oh boy, I really wanted to be Zachary Manly then: I wanted my legs to stop knocking together when I talked to Maia; I wanted his body - thick legs, high chest, wide arms; I wanted his confidences; I wanted...

"Attention, I Zachary Manly challenge you to a fight." He ran to the bed, jumped on top of me, and jabbed my chest hard. I started to cry and somehow managed to get him off me. I couldn't take the pain, especially Zachary's punches.

I ran to the bathroom. Luckily, we were alone. So I didn't mind running through his house with just underwear on (white Fruit of the Loom). I turned on the light and stared at myself in the full length mirror hanging on the door.

"You are a wimp. Look at yourself," I said crying at the truth in front of me. The door opened, and Zachary stood smiling in his underwear (blue Fruit of the Loom).

"C'mon to bed."

I shook my head. Zachary shut off the light, grabbed my hand, bent down, and lifted me on top of his back. (Zachary always does that to make me feel happy, and last night he succeeded again).

I lay in bed, a foot away from Zachary, thinking of Orion in the sky. Suddenly, Zachary moved closer to me so that his body was almost touching mine. He was breaking one of our rules.

"Zach, you awake?"

He moved closer until his left arm was over my naked chest.

I opened my eyes, and Andrew, Maia and a crowd of jeering onlookers were in front of me.

"Get up. Fight like a man," Andrew screamed.

"Kiss me," Maia whispered.

I started to panic when, suddenly, Zachary kissed me (he really did) and Andrew, Maia, and those salivating onlookers were gone.

Well, needless to say, I was surprised at Zachary's action, but, most important, I was relieved: a kiss from by bed buddy and the nightmare was over.

❖❖❖❖❖❖❖❖❖❖❖❖❖❖❖❖❖❖❖❖❖❖❖❖❖❖❖❖❖

James Markides ❖ *"I am 25 years old. I hold a Bachelor of Arts degree with a double major in Philosophy and English. Recently completing my Bachelor of Education, I am in the process of doing my practicum. During this process, and in the future years as educator, I hope to 'spread the word' about lesbians and gays. One way to do this is through the medium of literature. The 'lesbigay voice' needs to speak and be heard."*
James writes short stories, essays, and poetry; has acted in theatre productions.

❖❖❖❖❖❖❖❖❖❖❖❖❖❖❖❖❖❖❖❖❖❖❖❖❖❖❖

Photo by Paul Hanson

Courtesy of the Paul Hennefeld Gay and Lesbian History On Stamps Collection

PAH poster and Tee-shirt photo reproductions by written permission of Pop Against Homophobia Director, Adrian Be.

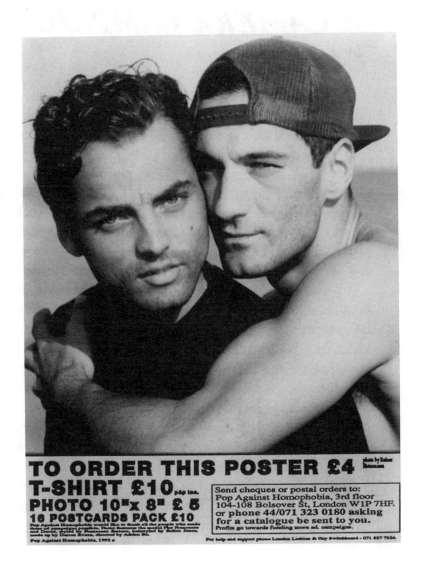

99

FLASHBACK OF A CAMERA CAMPAIGN

by Paul Hanson

After several years of independent study, a photographer friend of mine decided to take a formal class on photographic technique and composition at a Manhattan school known for turning out accomplished artists. While taking the course, my friend, Jim, had to compile a portfolio of photographs on some theme. Jim decided that his theme would be gay and lesbian couples. It took a great deal courage for Jim to seek approval of this theme - it was the late '80's - and once accepted, to show the work publicly. As he related the story for me, the acceptance of his work was rather astonishing to him.

I was really proud that he had chosen gay and lesbian couples as a theme from a political perspective. One of the biggest problems the lesgay rights movement faces is a lack of visibility. As I see it, it's a Catch 22 situation. The pervasive homophobia and institutionalized discrimination coupled with our ability to be invisible motivates us to be closeted. Yet, to overcome the homophobia and discrimination, we need to be visible. We need to show everyone that we are everywhere. We need to stand up for our own rights. However, the risks, depending on where we live and work, are so high.

I use my photography in photojournalistic ways to create visibility. I do this by illustrating newsletters of lesgay organizations, and to record events that might not be covered by the professional media. This has a place. But the kind of photography Jim has done is of enormous value - depicting gay and lesbian people in their lives and making those images available to the public is a component of a visibility campaign. It's a campaign that anyone with any camera can join. We should record who we are. We can put these pictures on our desks at work. We can enclose them with our holiday greeting cards to relatives. We can show faces on posters announcing lesgay activities. Images are powerful. They will be scutinized. They will have an impact.

❖❖❖❖❖❖❖❖❖❖❖❖❖❖❖❖❖❖❖❖❖❖❖❖❖❖❖❖❖

ABOUT THE AUTHOR

Paul Hanson ❖ *Born in 1960 in Cherry Hill, NJ, his primary interests while growing up were academics and the outdoors. He achieved the rank of Eagle Scout in the Boy Scouts of America Troop 144, and earned a B.S. in Electrical and Computer Engineering at Drexel University and a M.S. at Carnegie and Mellon University. He lives with his lover of seven years, Neil Ostroff, and is employed by AT&T Bell Laboratories. They enjoy high adventure backpacking trips and canoeing trips, sometimes with the Sundance Outdoor Adventure Society, a New York based gay/lesbian outing club. They look forward to the day when their nieces and nephews can join them on these adventures. Paul took up photography as a hobby in 1989. A Human Relations Commissioner, he joins with other minorities, law enforcement and community leaders to fight bias.*

❖❖❖❖❖❖❖❖❖❖❖❖❖❖❖❖❖❖❖❖❖❖❖❖❖❖❖❖❖

LIFESHARE

One winter, Colleen and I brainstormed
new and appropriate ways to sign our
holiday cards as a couple. We discounted
'lover' because that focused only on sex;
'partner' sounded too businesslike. What
we came up with was LIFESHARE, someone you share you life with. -Pat Freeman,
Editor, LAVENDER EXPRESS

102

FROM *ANOTHER MOTHER TONGUE* BY JUDY GRAHN

FROM THE CHAPTER TITLED, "FAIRIES AND FAIRY QUEENS"

— We never thought of ourselves as "Fairies," Vonnie, nor did we dream there had ever been such people as that, tribal Fairy people with Gay customs. Recently, I have been looking at pictures of you, my Von, and remembering how your ears stuck out. You wore your hair in such a way as to accentuate this feature and never to hide it. I believe you were as proud of your stuck-out ears as you were of your distinguished-looking salt-and-pepper hair. I am remembering how bright your eyes and smile were, what a lively, animated person you were. And how very short you kept your hair; how often you wore Levis and a turquoise inlaid cowboy belt even though it singled you out from other women so distinctly, and in such a butchy manner. You did this even while you scaled the professional ladder in your occupation. You could have been a conventionally handsome woman; instead, you chose to be handsome and at the same time clearly a dike, clearly a jester who kept conventional social situations slightly off-balance.

I am remembering how animatedly you handled your physical being. You talked with your hands and arms and with the rich up and down of your voice. I remember the gurgle of your laugh, as though a brook tumbled out of your mouth. I really took you for granted; I suppose we all do that with our first love. I idolized and adored you, and when I just took your special qualities for granted. After all, you were "mine" during those first years. since then I've not met anyone with the lively spirit you had, especially when you talked about ideas. You loved ideas the way people love flowers or babies or new electronic devices. You loved to talk for hours about the nature of ideas the way some people talk about cars or politics or their careers. You believed that teachers could teach students in public schools pure ideas and that the students would love it. You were a very intellectual Fairy, Von, and I think too far ahead of your time, weren't you? The pictures of you remind me of your great spirit, and how very funny you were in your way of talking, never cutting or cruel, never biting as I sometimes am. I don't remember a deliberately cruel or vindictive thing from you; you appeared baffled by those qualities in others. I remember you being witty and fun-loving the way we imagine a Fairy person ought to be.

BUT THIS is all a made up idea of what a "Fairy" might be. Usually the word isn't used about Lesbians, although sometimes it means Gay people in general. Nor is there any reason for women not to adopt the term for themselves once we know its meaning for Gay people. I have heard it most often as a derogatory term, indicating a certain kind of Gay man, meaning what PANSY means: effeminate, not rigidly masculine in manner. A circular path led me to the clues about why such a word is used about Gay people, beginning with another idea entirely: the color green.

NEVER WEAR GREEN ON THURSDAY

A people's culture does not exist as one big puddle into which everything flows indiscriminately. Like vast oceans, cultures have their own geography, currents and tides, pools and backwaters. The separate streams of culture flow together in multiple currents of classes, age groups, regions, and ethnic backgrounds, each adding a very specific variety to the whole

104

swirl of life.

Children recite and teach each other games and songs that may be hundreds, perhaps thousands, of years old. The cadences and stanzas were also chanted by children in sixteenth-century London or Moscow, in medieval France or Tunis, in ancient Jerusalem or Goa. What may be true, or "known," when a person is one age may never be known again in the same lifetime. Many children's games and saying belong only to them, as part of a children's subculture; adults do not play the games and may no longer be aware of their content. London's bridge has been falling down for many generations of American children who live far from London and far from any understanding of the event. In 1975, Black children on my block in Oakland sang a modern version: "London's britches falling down," and so the song spins on, still alive and meaningful...

What was of most immediate, excruciating interest were the increasing references, among the Anglo students at least, to "queers" and "fairies" that began to surface in the ninth grade and gradually intensified as we were pressured into pairing off for the purpose of marriage. Ninth graders repeated the words with a contempt not related to whether anyone really understood the definition. The animosity was apparently what mattered. In sophomore and junior years, when most of us were sixteen and seventeen, a new element was added to the generalized baiting of queers. It became suddenly a known "fact" that anyone who wore the color green on a Thursday was automatically a queer or a fairy. This puzzling, illogical formula was repeated dozens of times throughout the school year...

ANOTHER MOTHER TONGUE; GAY WORDS, GAY WORLDS,

(c) 1984 by Judy Grahn   Beacon Press.

105

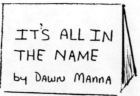

Faggot - A bundle of sticks
bound together;
bundle of steel RODS-
bind in a Faggot.

Dyke: Dike- Ditch: low wall, embankment -
wall or Ditch

Queen- Wife of a king,
Female sovereign,
Perfect female bee,
wasp, court card.

So what do
you guys think
About that?

Come on guys
she's JUST A
Know-IT-All.

Now THAT'S
A NAME I
COULD LIVE
WITH.

"EDUCATION PREVAILS"

108

❖◆❖◆❖◆❖◆❖◆❖◆❖◆❖◆❖◆❖◆❖◆❖◆❖◆❖◆❖◆❖◆❖

About the Cartoonist

Dawn Manna ❖ *Originally from the New Jersey area, Dawn is a free lance cartoonist. Her work includes (JAZZ) THE ADOLESCENT LESBIAN found only in the L-CONNECTION of South Florida. Also in the works, "EARTH GODDESS" soon to appear in THE FOUNTAIN MAGAZINE. She is a member of the Lesbian Cartoonist Network. DAWN MANNA PRODUCTIONS has also been published in THE ADVOCATE MAGAZINE, THE COMMUNITY VOICE, LANA'S WORLD, and several local newspapers. Dawn has created her own line of greeting cards which are sold at many feminist book stores throughout the nation. She now resides in South Florida with her lover, Cory, the only woman she has ever loved.*

❖◆❖◆❖◆❖◆❖◆❖◆❖◆❖◆❖◆❖◆❖◆❖◆❖◆❖◆❖◆❖◆❖

109

PART III

VISION

Creating Curriculum in Lesbigay Culture

Excerpts from

PROJECT 10 HANDBOOK

Addressing Lesbian and Gay Issues In Our Schools - A Resource Directory for Teachers, Guidance Counselors, Parents and School-Based Adolescent Care Providers

(PROJECT 10 is a high school on-campus counseling program organized in 1984 in response to the unmet needs of adolescent lesbians/gays in the educational system. The focus of the model is education, reduction of verbal and physical abuse, suicide prevention, and accurate AIDS information).

Section on Lesbian and Gay Minorities

...The various cultures and races reflected in the United States are also reflected in the lesbian and gay population. Such adolescents face the prospect of living their lives within three rigidly defined strongly independent communities: the lesbian and gay community, their ethnic or racial community, and the society at large. Each community fulfills basic needs which are often imperiled if such communities were to be visibly integrated. A common result is the constant effort to maintain a manner of living that keeps the three communities separate, a process that leads to increased isolation, depression and anger centered around the fear of being separated from all support systems including the family.

A unique feature of the ethnic family constellation is that it centers around the integration of the extended family within its support system. The ethnic family support system resembles more of a tribe with multiple family groups rather than a nuclear family structure consisting solely of parents and children. For the ethnic person the family constitutes a symbol of their basic roots and the focal point of their ethnic identity. "Coming out" to the family is a different process for the ethnic gay and lesbian than for the non-ethnic person since such a process tends to involve more than just the nuclear family.

FRIENDS OF PROJECT 10 (c) 1989

...Discrimination on the basis of sexual orientation is often compounded by economic disadvantage. The ethnic person is a visible minority and, therefore is more easily subjected to discrimination policies. Among blacks and Hispanics, employment discrimination is often present despite the level of education, academic degrees and years of employment. Further, unemployment rates are higher among some minority groups adding the burden of poverty, drug and alcohol abuse to quality of interaction among ethnic lesbians and gays...School personnel need to recognize the issues that exist and work toward understanding cross cultural differences.

Belinda

Most of my friends call me "Bee," but my name is Belinda. I am a 17 year old black lesbian and senior at Fairfax High School. Many many think that it is easy and perhaps not important, but coming from a person with a lifetime of experience, I know what it's like to grow up in the black community.

There are many complications in the black community -- drugs, gangs, no place to go, nothing exciting to do. This is everyday life for me -- going to school and going home.

Being 17 doesn't help much. I'm either too old to play with my brother or too young to hang out with my sister. I have to listen to what my mother says, yet develop a life of my own. This is where my lesbianism is modified.

I've always had feelings of being a lesbian, but being in a black Baptist family, it wasn't much talked about. Yet when it was, it wasn't condemned. I had a lot of play "uncles" who were gay, but I never knew what it was until I started recognizing my own feelings. This is when I became distant from friends and family. I didn't talk to my family a lot, because I was afraid that something might slip, or what's

112

worse, that they would ask me about a boyfriend. Friends were really a problem because boys are all that young girls my age discuss.

I didn't know what being a lesbian was all about or if it was o.k. so I didn't talk to anyone about it or tell any of my friends what I was feeling. I became non-social in school and spent most of my time in the library. I basically stayed by myself. I was more comfortable that way. At least I thought I was until I started feeling lonely.

One day I told a friend of mine that I was a lesbian. I thought that she could deal with it, and did for a while. A few days after talking about me and discussing our differences, she wrote me a letter. The letter so so harsh. She told me that she no longer wanted to be my friend. I was so hurt. I had experienced the rejection that my other gay friends talked about.

In the community where I lived, there was nothing clean or safe for young black lesbians to do. All the desired things such as rap groups, dances, plays, and youth centers were in West Hollywood, and without a car, the activities were hard to reach. So what I began to do was read. I would read lesbian fiction novels and also documentary books that gave me the feeling of not being alone. PROJECT 10 also played an important part in my maturing. It helped build my self-esteem and gave me a positive direction in which to go. I began to participate in school activities such as the Westchester High School health fair. I sat at a PROJECT 10 booth, shared with the Gay and Lesbian Community Services Center along with two other lesbians. It was a very nice experience. I was able to answer questions that students asked. I also learned that people are eager to learn more about homosexuality, but because the information is not available, they tend to be scared of the unknown.

Now, as part of my lesbian and feminist calling, I want to try to encourage and help more of the young lesbians in the black community to feel and know that it is "o.k." to be a lesbian. I would like to start a gay community center in the black community so that we won't have to leave home to be accepted. But also, it will allow us to grow together as one, not only to stregthen the black community but also to know more about homosexuality. Perhaps one day it will be accepted as a special thing rather than as a fault.

INTERVIEW WITH LESTER WONG AND LILLIAN GEE

LESTER: So I went to my mother who was asking me why wasn't I dating a girl? And why I wasn't planning on getting married, and was I going to get married?

And I tried to explain to her in Chinese, 'cause she doesn't speak English, that I'm gay. And the way I had to do it was to say, "Ma, I love men."

And her reaction was, "I don't care if you love men, you still have to get married."

I grew up in Chinatown and all my friends were Chinese until I decided to "come out." And coming out meant leaving and knowing that you couldn't get support from your friends or community...and not even trying because you're afraid to ask. And trying to go to a white gay (community)...and trying to fit in there. It didn't work.

LILLIAN: In Asian culture I have my role as a woman, but their is no role at all for me as a lesbian. I think outside of Chinatown, in white America, it's a much more violent opposition to gay people...it's a much more actively negative thing to be gay.

114

LESTER: Growing up as a little Chinese kids--all those ignorant
                ideas--these people calling me "fag" for no reason at
                all--it was a racial thing. They needed someone to
                dump on and they used the words "fag," "queer," and
                "sissy," on me because I was Chinese.

LILLIAN: I think that's the way racism and homophobia came
                from-- exactly the same fears on the part of whites.
                And so they use a homophobia expression like
                "faggot" to really express a racial fear. (Taken from
                page 38 of Project 10--Pink Triangle documentary).

Self-Esteem Issues

A final area of which school personnel should be aware is the
general area of self-esteem. Not only do adolsecent homosexuals
hear constant rounds of verbal abuse...but they also internalize
negative attitudes which contribute to a highly diminished sense of
self-esteem. These attitudes are summarized so that teachers and
other school personnel can gain insight in the critical area of esteem
among lesbian and gay teenagers.

Perhaps because males are valued more than females in our
society and male events are viewed as more important than female
events, negative attitudes about homosexuality are more directed
toward males than females. Male heterosexuals are more negative
toward male homosexuals than toward lesbians. There is also a
prevalent but erroneous view that homosexuals behave like the
opposite sex. Therefore, males are often taunted mercilessly by their
classmates...Often males who are experiencing same-sex feelings will
refuse to go to P.E. classes, and this will be the first thing that brings
them to the attention of their counselor.

...Although lesbians do not always suffer the type of overt discrimination found among gay males, their self-esteem is severely damaged by the sexism present in our society as well as the self-hatred they internalize as lesbians. Data suggests that lesbians do not express themselves as early as gay males. For that reason, the high school years may be especially confusing with regard to their sexuality. Counselors should be aware of this and alert for signs of isolation and depression. Often, teenage lesbians will not show the type of outward stress symptoms that are exhibited by gay males. As a result, they may be overlooked or trivialized.

The importance of counteracting negative feelings on the part of lesbian and gay teenagers cannot be overstressed. Young homosexuals must have positive images to which they can relate in order to reverse their sense of diminished self-esteem. Whenever possible, leaders of the lesbian and gay community should be identified and invited to speak to classes. Appropriate literature should be made available, as well as examples of positive role models. It is also important to discuss elements that people look for in establishing good relationships.

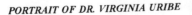

Dr. Virginia Uribe ❖ *Project 10 founder, veteran teacher/counselor for LA United School District, has been at Fairfax High School since l959. Dr. Uribe received her PhD in Psychology, Sierra University. Has counseled hundreds of young men and women, getting daily calls from runaway or throwaway youth. Has spoken at schools throughout the nation - NYC, Nebraska, Virginia. Oregon, NJ, Washington, DC, and Canada.*

PORTRAIT OF DR. VIRGINIA URIBE

PROJECT 10
THE MODEL CONCEPT

EDUCATION

Sensitization and awareness training of staff.

Direct liaison with counselors, school nurse and school psychologist regarding
special needs of lesbian and gay youth.

Expansion of the school library in both fictional and nonfictional areas. Removal
of perjorative material on homosexuality.

Development and coordination of a speaker's bureau.

SCHOOL SAFETY

School environment free of harassment and intimidation of sexual minorities.

Staff members trained in methods of recognizing and responding to victims of sexual
harassment.

Backup system developed so that incidents are reported and acted upon swiftly.

DROPOUT PREVENTION STRATEGIES

Informal rap groups, drop-in counseling and peer counseling experiences.

Inclusion of the lesbian and gay perspective in existing suicide and substance abuse prevention
programs.

Youth programs that give affirmative social experiences.

SUPPORT SERVICES

Accessibility to community resources.

Referrals to mental health personnel for in-depth counseling.

Private sector.

Human resources agencies.

Hotlines.

GLAAD (c) 1989   117

THE EQUITY INSTITUTE -
excerpts from STICKS, STONES, AND STEREOTYPES

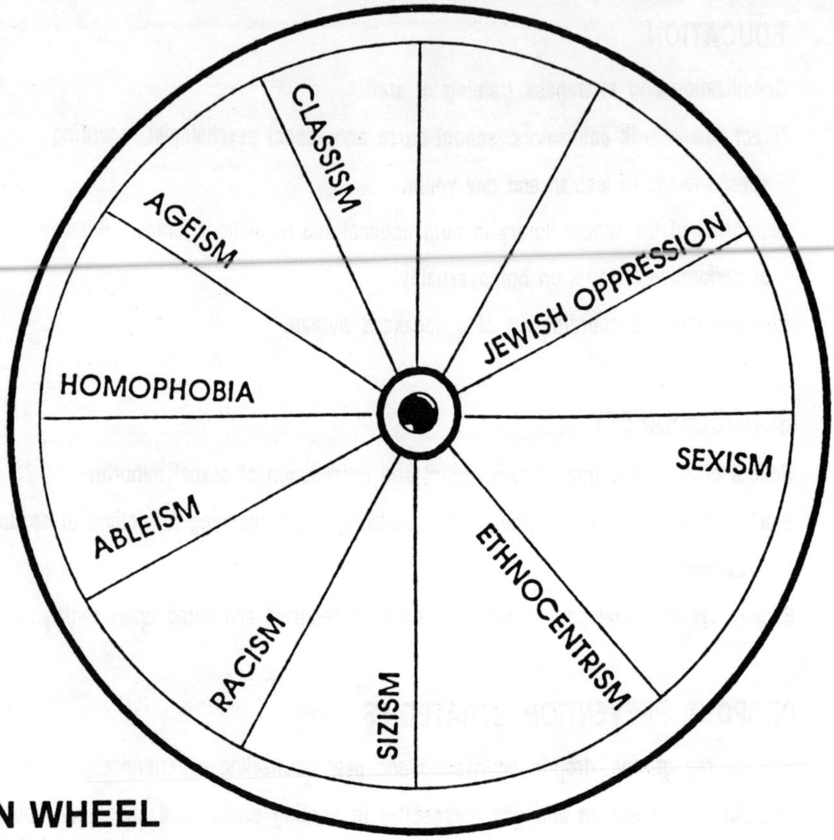

CLASSISM
JEWISH OPPRESSION
SEXISM
ETHNOCENTRISM
SIZISM
RACISM
ABLEISM
HOMOPHOBIA
AGEISM

OPPRESSION WHEEL

OPPRESSION

- the systematic subjugation of a disempowered social group by a group with access to social power

- or prejudice and power

PREJUDICE

- a set of negative beliefs, generalized about a whole group of people

SOCIAL POWER

- access and availability to resources needed to get what you want and influence others

PREJUDICE + POWER = "ISM"

INTRODUCTION
Sex-role stereotyping is extremely harmful to all human beings. As young people search for and develop their own identities, sex role stereotyping can seriously impede growth and achievement of individual potential. Namecalling and labeling are obstacles most young people face if they choose social, academic or athletic activities which run counter to gender stereotypes. Career choices are also often severely limited.

The messages of sex-role stereotyping are clear. Babies are color-coded from birth. The pink or blue blanket in which a baby is wrapped to leave the hospital is a subtle but clear symbol, a message which continues to limit in hundreds of ways as the baby grows into a young man or woman. And what if the child or the young adult chooses to step outside of the stereotypes? What if the young man chooses to become a hairdresser, a nurse or a homemaker? What if the young woman chooses to become a football player, a truck driver or a firefighter? What are the labels, names and stereotypes these young people face because they choose to explore and follow their own interests and areas of strength?

In order to eliminate these harmful sex-role stereotypes, it is essential to do away with homophobia and heterosexism. They are woven together and part of the same fabric. Sex-role stereotypes are rigidly held in place by homophobia. We contend that it is most often out of the fear of being labeled gay or lesbian that people follow rigid sex-role stereotypes.

Heterosexual people suffer a great deal from this in other ways. Adult same-sex closeness is almost always suspect, especially if there is any evidence of physical affection, e.g.. hugs, holding hands, kisses. As a result, many heterosexual people are not completely free to form close relationships with same-sex friends.

The effect of sex-role stereotyping on gays and lesbians is clearly and directly harmful. Rigid stereotypes imply that gay men are not "really men" and lesbians are "not really women." For young people who are searching for self-identity, this can be devastating.

The high incidence of gay-related youth suicides is clear evidence that sex-role stereotyping and homophobia are serious issues that cannot be ignored. Current research estimates that gay and lesbian youth comprise thirty to thirty-five percent of youth suicides annually. The reasons for this alarming statistic are directly related to the fact that many young people have stepped outside of traditional sex-role stereotypes. As a result, they are sometimes harassed, abused, assaulted and rejected by their friends, churches, synagogues and even their families. Suicide for these teenagers is a direct result of homophobia.

This is an important exercise. It will challenge students to examine their own self-imposed sex-role stereotypes. They will understand how homophobia affects their choices. Use this exercise to empower your students. Help them to see that there really are no limits to their success as full human beings.

GOAL
Students will gain a better understanding about the harmful impact of sex-role stereotyping and its correlation to homophobia

119

TIME   One class (45 minutes)

INSTRUCTIONS

1. Ask students to define:
- **SEX-ROLE STEREOTYPING**
- **HOMOPHOBIA**
- **HETEROSEXISM**

Brainstorm three definitions as a whole group.
Write the definitions on the blackboard.

Definitions we use at the Institute are:
SEX-ROLE STEREOTYPING: The assumption that males and females are limited by gender in their interests, capabilities and accomplishments. It is the assumption that being a man or woman, biologically limits what one can do as a human being.

HOMOPHOBIA: The fear or hatred of gays/lesbians or bisexuals; or the fear of same-sex closeness.

HETEROSEXISM: The assumption that everyone is heterosexual; that only heterosexuality is normal and therefore, superior.

IMPORTANT: Remember, at least ten percent of your class is gay/lesbian. Be careful not to refer to gays/lesbians as "others" and do not assume all of your students are heterosexual. Keep this in mind as you lead discussions.

2. Ask students to work in small groups of three for ten minutes. Their task will be to make a list of:

   a. all the things that only boys/men can do or are supposed to do

   b. all the things that only girls/women can do or are supposed to do

Explain that these two lists should reflect what students have been taught, either directly or indirectly by parents, teachers, siblings, and friends. The lists should not reflect what students actually know to be true. They should reflect stereotypes.

3. Ask each group to report out (adding only what has not already been stated from other groups). Compile two master lists: one for males and one for females on the blackboard as students report out.

4. Discuss the ways that sex-role stereotyping hurts all human beings: men and women. Ask students to give examples of ways they have stepped outside of traditional sex-role stereotypes in their lives.

5. Give information about the correlation between sex-role stereotyping and homophobia. Explain the relationship, and clarify that sex-role stereotyping will exist as long as homophobia exists.

6. Ask students to name the ways that homophobia hurts them. Brainstorm with the whole group (briefly). Point out that these are the same ways sex-role stereotyping hurts all of us, by limiting us in our choices. Point out that this is true whether we are gay/lesbian, bisexual or heterosexual.

120

> **7.** Ask students to work in small groups again to develop specific actions they might take to eliminate homophobia in the school (ten minutes in small groups).
>
> **8.** Ask students to report out. Record the actions on the board.
>
> **9.** APPRECIATIONS. Be sure to include . You may ask males to appreciate females and females to appreciate males. Do this as a whole group verbal exercise.

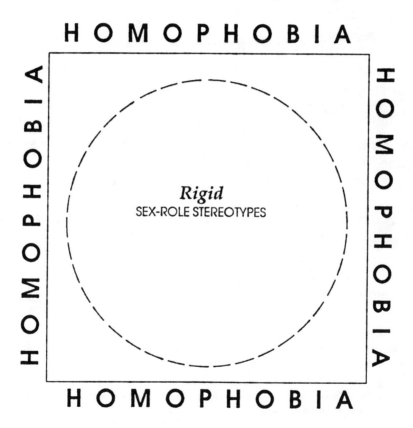

HOMOPHOBIA
HOMOPHOBIA
HOMOPHOBIA
HOMOPHOBIA

Rigid
SEX-ROLE STEREOTYPES

TRAPPED IN A BOX?!!

Counseling and Guidance Approaches
STAFF SURVEY

1. Do you think heterosexism and homophobia* are important issues for our students? _____Yes _____No

2. Have you ever had a conversation or incident in which you discussed this topic with students? If so, please describe briefly.

3. Are you aware that incidents of heterosexism and homophobia occur in this school? _____Yes _____No

    If yes, how often do you think?
    ___everyday___every week___once in a while___hardly ever
    Please give an example of one incident of which you have personal knowledge.

4. Do you need more information about how to work with students on this issue in school? _____Yes _____No
    If yes, what kind of information do you need?

5. Do you think your students understand the connections between racism, sexism and homophobia? _____Yes _____No

6. Should heterosexism/homophobia be addressed in an ongoing way through identified school curriculum? _____Yes _____No

7. Would you be involved in developing methods to educate about and interrupt incidents of heterosexism and homophobia? If so, please contact me.

*HOMOPHOBIA: The fear of same-sex closeness, translated into fear or hatred of gays and lesbians.
*HETEROSEXISM: The assumption that everyone is heterosexual, and that only heterosexuality is normal. and therefore superior.

122

⌘⌘⌘⌘⌘⌘⌘⌘⌘⌘⌘⌘⌘⌘⌘⌘⌘⌘⌘⌘⌘⌘⌘⌘⌘⌘⌘⌘⌘⌘⌘⌘⌘⌘⌘⌘⌘

TIPS FROM THE PINK PANTHERS
SEE US, RESPECT US

The Pink Panthers, a special patrol force of lesbians and gays in NYC who patrol the streets to deter bashing say-

- if you are a student in school and name calling occurs, instead of withdrawal or confrontation, simply reply, "Yes, I AM queer, SO WHAT?

- Do NOT put your head down; show self-determination in your body language.

- talk to your guidance counselor or parent regarding such encounters.

- if you are walking on the street, be aware of the people around you (especially clusters of male youth 15-22; statistics show this age group commits an inordinate amount of violence based on prejudice).

- when sensing impending confrontation, cross the street or slacken your walk and let them pass. FIND A SAFE SPOT.

RECOMMENDATIONS FOR YOUR SCHOOL *by Gail Watnick*

Everyone contributes to a happier, healthier school environment.

THE SCHOOL COUNSELOR

A school counselor can be the first in a school system to make alienated, confused students feel less marginalized and more content to participate in the high school experience. A counselor can give reassurance, and an opportunity for the youth to speak openly.

Be sure counselors examine their own feelings about homosexuality, and recognize that the American Psychiatric Association ceased to catagorize it as an illness in 1973. Adolescents are oftimes very perceptive to attitudes. Remember, one is not "advocating" a lesbian or gay existence; instead, the counselor could be neutral or positive enough to acknowledge that being lesbian or gay comes as natural as breathing the air for 10% of the student body.

School counselors can place informative, unbiased books, posters and pamphlets in their offices and discuss it with those who inquire. Discussions can include family and peers.

124

THE LIBRARIAN

The school librarian can play a large part in a healthy adolescent development. The library has access to funds and the ability to obtain helpful resources for its students. The librarian, however, must be willing to do a bit of research, and be aware that negative, as well as positive literature exists.

A few practical suggestions include:

1. The library should adopt books which portray the central characters as heroes who also happen to be homosexual. Books might also include descriptions of falling in love in the same way that heterosexual couples are portrayed.

2. Be aware of how a student would go about finding material; recognize that a derogatory first impression could turn a student away from obtaining accurate information. One place most turn to is the encyclopedia or dictionary. Libraries should have updated encyclopedias that portray the healthfulness of homosexuality.

3. Use neutral terms in the card catalogue when describing books with lesbian or gay themes.

Happy reading!

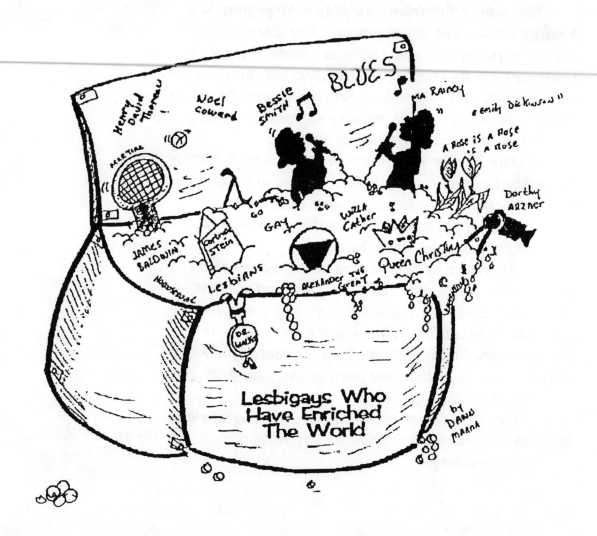

126

A CULTURALLY DIVERSE LOOK
Reasons to Include Lesbian and Gay History in Schools by Dell Richards

There are three reasons for including lesbians and gays in textbooks and school curricula. **First, of course, is accuracy.** As educators, it is very important that we tell the truth to the best of our ability. And certainly, plenty of lesbians and gay men are already in courses of study. We recognize that many are pathfinders, superstars, people who have enriched society. But what we are not told is their sexuality. For instance, Walt Whitman, one of America's most famous poets, not only celebrated the common man, but also celebrated the eroticism of the male. If you read his poetry through gay eyes, you will realize this. The interpretation is very different once you take this into account. Another example, Jane Addams, the nineteenth century reformer and founder of Hull House, is a forerunner of the modern day lesbian movement and part of the Romantic Friends Movement. She gave all her energies to women: emotional, physical, political. She basically lived in a commune; she had her "steadies" and she also had her crushes.

For the most part, it is more difficult to verify the lives of lesbians. Usually, they didn't leave diaries explaining this. Or if they did, their relatives oftimes destroyed them. This was the case with American poet, Emily Dickinson, whose niece withheld her love letters to women, until now. Scholars have trotted out every male who crossed her path and said this was her love interest, when in fact she had three women in her life that she really did love. In addition, during the Victorian Era, sexuality wasn't discussed at all. Susan B. Anthony, known in the history books as a suffragette, was also precursor of the Romantic Friends Movement.

The second reason for cultural inclusion lies with the youth. **Lesbian and gay adolescents have one of the highest suicide rates, one of the**

127

highest drop out rates, and one of the highest substance abuse rates in the country. And quite understandably. If you grow up hearing about heterosexuals only, seeing movies, art, and literature in this framework, you end up thinking the whole world is heterosexual. And when you find out you're lesbian or gay, it's very terrifying to feel you are part of the most vilified minority in the world. And lesbian and gay youth's behavior show this. They have nobody to talk to. They don't want their friends to know. They can't talk to their parents, their teachers. They have virtually no positive, visible role models in history.

A third reason for inclusionary education is that **America prides itself on being a Melting Pot. That worthy goal goes beyond mere tolerance, to understanding one another, and celebrating the incredible diversity that we have.** We begin by opening our arms to every religious, every racial and every sexual minority. We need to include all of them in the social studies books - children of lesbians and gays, African Americans, Latinos, Asian Americans and Native Americans. We need to include them so that kids growing up within these minorities can feel as if they are part of the mainstream.

(This message was aired on OUTLOOKS, a GLIB Production, Pacifica Radio, NY, and On-The-Line, a Lesbian and Gay radio show in NJ.)

❖❖❖❖❖❖❖❖❖❖❖❖❖❖❖❖❖❖❖❖❖❖❖❖❖❖❖❖❖❖❖❖❖❖❖❖

Dell Richards ❖ *The author of LESBIAN LISTS, a fascinating look at lesbians through the centuries with more than 1,000 names and short biographies, ranging from lesbian writers and artists to rulers and aristocrats, actresses and directors, theorists and politicians, switchhitters and lesbians who passed as men. Dell has also contributed to YOU CAN DO SOMETHING ABOUT AIDS and has authored THE RAPE JOURNAL. A professional journalist, she is widely traveled and lived in London, Washington, DC and Los Angeles. Resides in Idaho*

❖❖❖❖❖❖❖❖❖❖❖❖❖❖❖❖❖❖❖❖❖❖❖❖❖❖❖❖❖❖❖❖❖❖❖❖

GLAAD: Gay and Lesbian Alliance Against Defamation

GLAAD is dedicated to fighting for fair, accurate and inclusive representations of lesbian and gay lives in the mass media - newspapers, magazines, films, radio, and T.V. THE GLAAD BULLETIN, a bimonthly newsletter in some regions, targets recent coverage of lesbigay issues, prompting their expansive readership to take appropriate action, recommending support, 'thank you' letters, telegrams of dissatisfaction, or even, boycott.

In 1989, GLAAD/LA prepared a teaching guide aimed at educating students about anti lesbian and gay prejudice. Used in conjunction with the Anti-Defamation League's "A World of Difference" campaign, this curriculum, titled, "Homophobia: Discrimination Based on Sexual Orientation," is comprised of five parts. "A Lesson In History," and "Preparing Your Class For Speakers On Homosexuality" (pages 129-136) are taken from this curriculum. One spokesperson explains the significance of this type of instruction: "It is important to deal with prejudice reduction directly in the education system. It is a mistake to think that schools only need to deal with reading, writing, and arithmetic."

A LESSON IN HISTORY

READING: 1. Historical Figures
2. Chronology of the Lesbian and Gay Movement (in the U.S.)

OBJECTIVES:
1. To introduce students to a few lesbians and gay men who have enriched the world.
2. To explain that same-sex oriented women and men have been present in many cultures, in all ages of history, and in all occupations.
3. To enable students to view the lesbian and gay movement in its historical context, permitting comparison with other civil rights movements.

129

GENERAL STATEMENT: The purpose of this lesson is to help the students become aware of same-sex oriented women and men in all cultures and as part of history. It is designed to challenge stereotyping or prejudice against homosexuals.

TEACHING STRATEGY: Ask students to read the two articles, "Historical Figures," and "Chronology of the Lesbian and Gay Movement."

DISCUSSION QUESTIONS:

1. Are there any names you recognize on the list of "Historical Figures"? Did you know that these people had lesbian or gay relationships? Now that you know their sexual orientation do you find anything different about the way you feel?

2. What do you think about history books that omit personal information about prominent figures, such as their race, national origin, religion or sexual orientation?

3. Did you know that there was a history in this country of lesbians and gay men striving for equality?

ACTIVITY: 1. Have students prepare reports on an historical figure of their choice. The students may not necessarily find references to the firgures' sexual orientation. Why have these references been omitted? Should they be included?

2. Have students pick a specific incident from the chronology of the lesbian and gay movement and research it. They may also choose to research a lesbian and gay organization which emerged at this time, or to compare the lesbian and gay movement with other civil rights movements.

HISTORICAL FIGURES:

According to many sources, numerous historical figures were involved in same-sex relationships. Many lesbian and gay men hid their sexual orientation fearful of the persecution and prejudice to which they would have been subjected. Even many of the famous figures listed below who were open regarding their sexual orientation are not generally identified as such; this aspect of their lives was censored/omitted from history. This list, by no means exhaustive, will give the reader a feeling for the tremendous

130

contributions to our culture made by lesbians and gay men. The sexual orientation of those listed below has been documented by their own work, discussions about their lives, or other historical data.

Sappho	600 BC	Greek philosopher, poet
Alexander the Great	356-323 BC	Macedonian ruler
Plato	427-347 BC	Greek philosopher
Julius Caesar	100-44 BC	Roman emperor
Hadrian	76-138 AD	Roman emperor
Richard the Lion-Hearted	1157-1199	English king
Richard II	1367-1400	English king
Leonardo da Vinci	1452-1519	Italian artist, inventor
Desiderius Erasmus	1466-1536	Dutch monk, philosopher
Michelangelo	1475-1626	Italian artist
Montezuma II	1480-1520	Aztec ruler
Francis Bacon	1561-1626	English statesman, author
Christopher Marlowe	1564-1593	English writer
Queen Christina	1626-1689	Swedish queen
Peter the Great	1672-1725	Russina czar
Fredrick the Great	1712-1786	King of Prussia
Madame de Stael	1766-1817	French writer
Lord Byron	1788-1824	English poet
Hans Christian Anderson	1805-1850	Danish author
Margaret Fuller	1810-1850	US writer, educator
Herman Melville	1819-1891	US author
Walt Whitman	1819-1892	US author
Horatio Alger, Jr.	1832-1899	US author, founder of orphanages
Peter Ilyich Tchaikovsky	1840-1893	Russian composer
We-Wha	? -1896	Zuni Indian leader

Oscar Wilde	1854-1900	Irish author
Marcel Proust	1871-1922	French author
Sergei Diaghileff	1872-1929	Founder of modern Russian ballet
Willa Cather	1873-1947	US author
Colette	1873-1954	French author
Amy Lowell	1874-1925	US poet
Gertrude Stein	1874-1946	US author, poet, collector of art
Renee Vivien	1877-1909	English poet
Alice B. Toklas	1877-1967	US author
E.M. Forster	1879-1970	English author
Radclyffe Hall	1880-1943	English author
Virginia Woolf	1882-1941	English author
John Maynard Keynes	1883-1946	English economist
T.E. Lawrence	1888-1935	English soldier, author
Ludwig Wittgenstein	1889-1951	Austrian mathematician
Jean Cocteau	1880-1963	French author, filmmaker
Vita Sachville-West	1892-1962	English author
Federico Garcia Lorca	1894-1936	Spanish poet, dramatist
Bessie Smith	1894-1937	Black American singer
Charles Laughton	1899-1962	English actor
Noel Coward	1899-1973	English author, composer
Margherite Yourcenou	1903-1987	French author, translator
Christopher Isherwood	1904-1986	English author
Tenessee Williams	1911-1983	US playwright
Benjamin Britten	1913-1976	English composer
Pier paolo Pasolini	1922-1975	Italian filmmaker
James Baldwin	1924-1987	Black American author
Yukio Mishma	1925-1970	Japanese author
Andy Warhol	1930-1987	US artist
Michael Bennett	1943-1987	US choreographer, musical theatre

CHRONOLOGY OF THE LESBIAN AND GAY MOVEMENT IN THE US (thru 1988)

YEAR	EVENT
1890's -	Beginnings of lesbian and gay social institutions in major cities.
1924	Society for Human Rights, first formally organized gay movement group in the US.
1945	Large numbers of lesbian and gay veterans of World War II settle in cities, greatly increasing the size of urban lesbian and gay communities.
1947-53	McCarthyism: purge of homosexuals from federal government; thousands lose their job.
1948	Kinsey Report published: first major survey detailing American homosexual behavior
1951	Mattachine Society formed in Los Angeles (grows to over 100 discussion groups in Southern California by 1953).
1954	ONE, the first magazine for the lesbian and gay community, published in LA.
1955	The Daughters of Bilitis, the first lesbian organization, is formed in San Francisco.
1958	US Supreme Court rules that ONE magazine may be sent through the mail (first US Supreme Court victory for the community.
1961	Illinois becomes the first state to decriminalize homosexuality between consenting adults in private.
1964	
1967-68	Gays march on LA Police Department, protesting arrests (first gay protest march in US)
1968	Emergence of support/social groups on college campuses such as the Student Homophile League at Columbia and NYU.
	Metropolitan Community Church founded by lesbian and gay Christians in LA.

1969	Riot in reponse to police harassment at Stonewall Bar in NYC. (Recognized as the beginning of the gay and lesbian liberation movement. Early focus was on securing right to congregate at bars or other public places without being arrested).
1971	Connecticut, Colorado and Oregon decriminalize homosexual acts.
	National Organization for Women acknowledges oppression of lesbians.
1973-74	Homosexuality no longer considered a mental disorder by the American Psychiatric Association.
1975	California decriminalizes homosexuality.
1977	Harvey Milk is elected to San Francisco Board of Supervisors (the first openly gay person elected to public office).
1978	California state senator John Briggs proposes an amendment to expel from school systems lesbians and gay men and those who support equal rights for lesbians and gay men. Voters defeat the proposition by 58% to 42%.
	Harvey Milk assassinated in San Francisco City Hall by ex-Supervisor Dan White (who also assassinates San Francisco Mayor George Moscone).
1979	First March on Washington for Gay Rights (200,000)
	Riots in San Francisco after Dan White convicted of the lesser charge of manslaughter rather than murder for the killing of Harvey Milk.
1982	Wisconsin becomes the first state to pass a wide-reaching law prohibiting discrimination against lesbians and gays.
1984	Project 10 established at Fairfax High School in LA (nation's first public high school counseling program aimed at the needs of lesbian and gay students).
1987	October 10-11, 2nd March on Washington for lesbian and gay civil rights -- the largest lesbian and gay gathering ever -- an estimated 500,000.
1988	National Education Association adopts resolution calling for every school district to provide counseling for students struggling with their sexual orientation.

PREPARING YOUR CLASS FOR SPEAKERS ON HOMOSEXUALITY

OBJECTIVES:

1. Students will be able to hear and evaluate different points of view.
2. Students will be able to recognize the difference between information based on fact rather than stereotype.
3. Students will be able to exchange information about homosexuality in a setting that is non-threatening.

TEACHING STRATEGY:

1. STEP ONE - PREPARATION

a. Obtain any necessasry approval forms from parents and administration.

b. Contact a local organization (or use own resources) to obtain speaker. This may be a human service organization, parent group or some other local support group.

c. Prior to the speaking day, announce to the students that these speakers will be coming. Share with your students the expectations and rules you have. Explain that the speakers are there to give information, break stereotypes, and so forth, but may feel it is inappropriate or unnecessary to talk about very personal matters.

d. Ask students to write down any questions they would like to ask the speakers. Review these questions and prepare a short list to give the speaker about the topics to be covered. Written questions can be solicited during or immediately before the speakers' presentation, collected, and then given to the speakers as part of the question and answer session. This is especially useful to the shyer students.

2. STEP TWO: SPEAKERS

a. Work out the format and presentation with the speakers prior to their arrival.

b. Be specific about what you want covered, and tell the speakers how you have prepared your students.

c. An invitation to speakers to talk about their every day life and goals can be among the most effective teaching methods. Although the students may be aware of gay men and lesbians, and may have members of their family who are homosexual, few have had the opportunity to talk freely with lesbians and gay men in a structured environment.

d. Same as much time as possible for verbal questions from the students. If questions are not forthcoming, perhaps you can draw upon these: Do their parents know that they are gay or lesbian? Were they "out" in high school? What was their high school experience like? When did they first have feelings that they might be gay or lesbian? What is the hardest part of being gay? How do they feel about speaking to a high school class?

e. Thank the speakers and the class for their participation.

3. STEP THREE: FOLLOW UP

a. The next day, have the students fill out a written eveluation sheet to be sent to the speakers.

b. Ask the students if they have any more questions on homosexuality.

c. Ask the students if they learned anything or cleared up any false notions they had about homosexuality as a result...

d. Discuss with the students the connection between misinformation and prejudice. Have their attitudes changed as a result.

e. Ask if the students think prejudice (of any minority) can be reduced by learning about groups that are oppressed?

(taken from HOMOPHOBIA, © 1989, a GLAAD, LA curriculum)

USING LESBIAN AND GAY READING SELECTIONS
WITH THE WHOLE LANGUAGE APPROACH Grades 7+
prepared by Sue McConnell-Celi

The Whole Language Approach is a holistic view of language education in which students integrate reading and writing skills, acquiring total information. It is student-centered and interactive, with participants learning to read or write as they engage in real literature and problem solving as opposed to individual, isolated tasks.

In a sense, it imitates life; for example, children speak long before they learn each individual letter of the alphabet.

It is important to utilize the growing number of fine lesbian and gay reading materials - novels, short stories, magazine and newspaper items - in your diversity lessons, so that everyone can acquire a more realistic comfort level. This subject is also valuable in building self-esteem in adolescent female students; oftimes lesbian-centered themes depict self-reliant, accomplished females, providing a much-needed role model for adolescents. One example (already read on the middle school level): Ann McGovern's THE SECRET SOLDIER, biography of Deborah Sampson, a woman who 'passes' as a man in order to join the Revolutionary Army. Students appreciate the heroine's sense of courage and independence.

Just as the general public is transforming into a more complete, accepting society, the educational community is adopting greater validation for each student's interpretation as the individual learner grows through analysis and understanding of a wide expanse of topics.

Sample Mini-Lesson

OBJECTIVES: Students develop critical reading/thinking skills by making use of stories that focus on examples of prejudice lesbian and gay teenagers encounter.
MATERIALS: THE HARD REALITY OF LATINA LESBIANS and THE STORY OF CHRIS (see Appendix for stories).

137

PROCEDURE:
1. *Copies of HARD REALITY... and STORY OF CHRIS distributed.*
2. *Teacher reads aloud while students read silently.*
3. *Follow up activities:*
   A. *Students respond in a daily DIALOGUE JOURNAL, writing comments.*
   B. *Discussion ensues as class or in "teams"; may focus on questions: "What role did prejudice play in each outcome? Have you ever witnessed such discrimination? How could these incidents have been avoided?"*
   C. *Poster Project: Materials distributed for creation of anti-lesbian/gay discrimination posters, glitter glue, magic markers, colorful posterboard. May employ advertising techniques (ie bandwagon approach, testimonial, etc). Post in corridors.*

FACT'PINION WORKSHEETS

OBJECTIVES: Participants differentiate between fact and opinion (or stereotype), comparing their views before and after the reading. Involves cooperation, group interaction, and good citizenship.

MATERIALS: Current newspaper editorials addressing the president's proposal to lift the ban on lesbians and gays in the military (or any timely topic - lesbigays having or adopting children; legally recording unions; sharing health benefits). Be selective when choosing materials; avoid negative or biased views, or at least maintain balanced coverage. Remember, we are attempting to gain understanding of the topic, not reinforce old labels. May also compare/supplement editorial statement with original news story (the 5 W's).

138

PROCEDURE:

1. Students form teams - groups of three or four. Each group assigns a recorder.
2. Fact'pinion sheets are distributed (sample page 141); members decide upon a few generalities about a current lesbigay topic. (ie: A student should come out to her parents... lesbians and gays contribute much to society...we should lift the ban on lesbians and gays in the military).
3. Recorder writes these general statements on the center line, marked 'general statements'.
4. The number of participants who agree are tallied in the space marked 'before'.
5. The newspaper/magazine editorial or article discussing this issue is distributed and read (teacher may read aloud to class while others silently read).
6. After readings, a brief discussion among group members may ensue.
7. Students re-evaluate their position, now tallied in the'after' column.
8. Results are then reported to the class by each group recorder.

PLOT CHART

OBJECTIVES: Readers recognize elements of plot, setting, and characterization.

MATERIALS: Full length novel selected from A BIBLIOGRAPHY; LESBIAN AND GAY ISSUES...(page 167).

PROCEDURE:

1. Distribute plot chart (sample page 141).
2. As the story progresses, students identify Setting (Time and Place); Characters (Describe- include orientation - main and supportive); Conflict or problem to overcome; Sequence of Main Events; and Conflict Resolution. Please note the importance of conflict resolution in the life of the teenager; it mirrors problems teens face and may serve to vicariously resolve them through books or on the screen - hence, afternoon TV theme specials for teens. Lesbian and gay youth - and girls, ages 9 and beyond - have the same needs to make confident, self-assuring decisions in a given situation.

POINT OF VIEW

OBJECTIVES: *Students decide the importance of writer's perspective or point of view. (Generally, would be helpful to define point of view, first-person narration, third-person narration - limited or omniscient - at this time).*

MATERIALS: *Novel or short story written by lesbian or gay person. Biographical information should be made available in objective fashion.*

PROCEDURE: *After reading, ask questions to promote connections: Who tells the story? Why might the author have decided to do it this way? What have I learned from the author's message? Does the author's perspective shed new light on what is happening? In what way(s) has the situation been viewed differently, if at all, through lesbian or gay eyes?*

☺☺

FIRST PERSON NARRATION

OBJECTIVES: *Participants examine a story of coming out, first-person experience.*

MATERIALS: *LEAVING CONFUSION BEHIND, a personal narrative about a high school student who discovers she has strong feelings for her best friend. (See Appendix).*

PROCEDURE: *The concept of "coming out" is discussed prior to reading. Upon story completion, teacher may ask the following questions: What was Gail's initial conflict? At the beginning of the story, did the narrator feel as if she were part of the group? Later, did this change? If so, why? Whom could she talk to about her uneasiness/conflict? What would you have done? Was the conflict resolved? Explain the title. Has the author's style of writing - use of dialogue, observation, surprise discovery - enhanced the story? (Note: it may be helpful for the teacher to become acquainted with literature on the coming out process by reading materials the school counselor or librarian may have. If these are not available, ask your administrator to order them. Remember, the teacher sets the tone for meaningful discussion).*

For Additional Curricula, see Respect For Diversity: Building Bridges in the Appendix

FACT'PINION SHEET

BEFORE	*GENERAL STATEMENT*	*AFTER*

☺☺☺☺☺☺☺☺☺☺☺☺☺☺☺☺☺☺☺☺☺☺☺☺☺☺☺☺☺☺☺☺☺☺☺☺☺☺☺

PLOT CHART

SETTING (TIME AND PLACE):

CHARACTER DESCRIPTION:
  Main:

  Secondary:

CONFLICT (Internal/External Problem to Overcome):

SEQUENCE OF MAIN EVENTS:

CONFLICT RESOLUTION:

141

PARALLELS IN HISTORY
Anne Frank ~ Introduction and Music
by Lynn Lavner

In 1987 I was invited to perform at the 10th World Conference of Gay and Lesbian Jews in Amsterdam. I stayed on after the conference to do some touring and was housed with a wonderful lesbian activist. I told her I planned on visiting the Anne Frank House. Her instant response was, "Let's go out in the backyard and have some tea and I'll tell you what I know to enhance your visit. You see, my mother went to school with Margot Frank, Anne's older sister.

I was both excited and struck with actually meeting someone connected with history, something you only read about in books.

Later that year, the Dutch government honored a Dutch Christian woman named Miep Gies. The employee of Anne Frank's father, Otto Frank, Miep was the woman who brought books, music, candy, and food that she somehow managed to scrounge up on the black market everyday to keep up the spirits of those who had been in hiding. This she did at great personal risk to herself. When government representatives contacted her, although she is a private person, she felt that it was important for the world never to forget these times. She made this statement: "I am not a hero; I only did what any decent person would have done under similar circumstances." And so for me, when I came home from Amsterdam, I knew I would write about Anne Frank. The song in the album, YOU ARE WHAT YOU WEAR (Bent label), was dedicated to Meip Gies.

I feel very strongly that there are parallels between that historical period and what happens to all oppressed minorities, particularly in the early days of the AIDS epidemic. (In the early days of AIDS, if medical science had begun researching and educating the public, we may be looking at a cure today, and undoubtedly fewer people with AIDS).

142

In 1989, I became the first foreign performer invited to the Netherlands to perform at their first Gay Pride Celebration. (Apparently ANNE FRANK, the new song, had gotten some air play over there). Miep Gies, a woman now well into her 80's, but who had remained active, was invited to attend Gay Pride as an honored guest. A few days before my departure, I received this note:

-- We thank you very much for your letter and for the excellent record.

Also, for the invitation to come to Holland, but there is disappointment for us.

The whole month of June we are on vacation in Switzerland.

-Miep

This letter is one of the belongings that I treasure the most.

❖❖

Lynn Lavner ❖ *Composer and entertainer, Lynn spends her time playing clubs, colleges, and concert halls across the US and Europe. Her earlier albums, "Something Different" and "I'd Rather Be Cute," are also available on BENT records and tapes. What about her unexpected popularity at gay religious events? "My father was a cantor," she explains, "so I simply regard my life as a very weird version of THE JAZZ SINGER."*
Most of her songs involve humor. She says, "My first loyal following in NYC comprised mostly gay men, and I learned to camp with the best of them. The female audience came a bit later..." Had been asked to play the National Women's Music Festival AND International Mr. Leather, all in the same year. Her latest performance - the '93 MARCH ON WASHINGTON!

❖❖

HELP SPREAD AWARENESS FOR BREAST CANCER AND AIDS

ORDER YOUR PINK & RED RIBBON PIN FROM SCWU TODAY

(AND DON'T FORGET TO ORDER SOME FOR FRIENDS AND GIFTS)

The Pink & Red Ribbon is a new symbol that promotes equal awareness of AIDS and the women's health crisis of breast cancer. The red portion of the ribbon represents the fight against AIDS. The pink section of this enamel pin signifies the crisis proportions of breast cancer: one in eight women will get breast cancer; half of them will die. Developed by The Center in Los Angeles, the symbolic pin is available from SCWU—which will use the proceeds to educate lesbians about AIDS, breast cancer and other women's health issues.

RIBBONS OF REMEMBRANCE Permission to reprint ad from SCWU (South California Chapter of the National Association of Women For Understanding, 1017 No. La Cienega Blvd., Suite 106, West Hollywood, Ca 90069)

Anne Frank
music and lyrics by Lynn Lavner

My world is bigger than this annex,
It's wider than this door,
And it's louder than the tiptoes that I take across this floor.
It's a world of books and music,
Decent women, decent men,
And if God is only willing, I will see my world again.
Looking back on all the months of keeping mum
We saw the signs of things to come.

First forbidden in the theaters,
Prohibited from sports,
Restricted in the shops, deprived of justice in the courts.
Then relieved of cars and bicycles,
Banned from trans and trains,
You're a foreigner in your city, you're a prisoner when it rains,
While a billion decent people held their breath
We learned that silence equals death.

Where is the voice of the people?
Why aren't they taking our part?
I still believe that people are really good at heart.

But they came and took our neighbors,
Nearly everyone we knew,
The ones who felt above it all, well, they were taken, too.
And we became the lucky ones,
Befriended, tucked away,
If you think about the others, you could sit and cry all day.
With the sky engulfed in darkness how it seems
I see the future now in dreams.

144

Where are the lessons in history?
Where are the visions of men?
Who doesn't learn from history will re-live it once again.

My world is bigger now than heaven,
It's a miracle of blue,
I'm a very famous writer, so you see my wish came true.
And you say, "The world is safe now. Be thankful and rejoice."
You believe that human preference is a private, personal choice.
Well, some of us know better
From the nightmare of our days,
You haven't had potatoes 'til you've had them fifty ways.
And tonight when you go sleepless,
Wondering whom to thank,
Toss among the bedclothes remembering Anne Frank.
Remember Anne Frank.

"ANNE FRANK" (c) 1988 by Lynn Lavner on the Bent Album

GAY AND LESBIAN HISTORY ON STAMPS CLUB
by Paul Hennefeld

There weren't too many visible gay heroes to look up to in the '30's and '40's. All too often, lesbian and gay writers were ignored by the public, their works were distorted or destroyed. Until recently - we are now beginning to recapture our heritage. It was Jonathan Katz' GAY AMERICAN HISTORY (Harper Row Publishers) that inspired me to compile a list of gays and lesbians on stamps. By co-founding the Gay and Lesbian History on Stamps Club - along with Blair O'Dell, my life partner, and Brian Lanter, we were able to break through the homo/lesbophobic barrier.

The first exhibit was in NYC, 1983. Since then, the collection has been shown throughout the US and Canada. This resulted in being granted Study Unit status of the American Topical Association (no easy feat!), 1985.

In 1989, I was proud to be asked by the US Post Office Department to assemble a 16-page exhibit about our club...

I have always been disturbed by publishers and Hollywood producers who deliberately distort or ignore our lesbian and gay history, consequently making our culture non-existant. Through my stamp collection, I hope to correct, in some small way, these injustices and falsehoods.

Recently, I was asked to be in the Court of Honor at the Jacob Javits Center, NYC for which I received a Gold Award (my tenth). I have also briefly appeared in a BBC documentary in a segment titled: CAMP STAMPS.

OUT OF THE CLOSET

OUT OF THE CLOSET designed by Marie Hochman for Paul Hennefeld
photo by Paul Hanson

ALEXANDER HAMILTON

Hamilton & Laurens

Hamilton wrote:

I wish my dear Laurens, it might be in my power by action rather than words, to convince you that I love you...like a jealous lover, when I thought you alighted my caresses, my affection was alarmed and my vanity piqued ...

The Surrender of Lord Cornwallis at Yorktown
From a Painting by John Trumbull

Photo by Paul Hanson
Courtesy of the Paul Hennefeld Gay and Lesbian History On Stamps Collection

Photo by Paul Hanson

Courtesy of the Paul Hennefeld Gay and Lesbian History On Stamps Collection

149

AUTHORS & POETS

Sappho of Lesbos, composed romantic verse extolling her love for women.
Desiderius Erasmus was accused of seducing his English pupil.
William Shakespeare wrote 154 'love sonnets' to Mr. W. H.

Banished from France for her political views, Madame Germaine de Staél
settled in Switzerland with her lover Madame Juliette Recamier.

Giacomo Leopardi shared a room with his friend Ranieri, despite the fact
separate rooms were rented.
Franz Grillparzer's diary revealed his affairs with two gentlemen.
Lord Byron's bisexuality is well known and documented.
Heinrich von Kleist wrote many love letters to the Prussian war minister,
Ernst von Pfuell.

Photo by Paul Hanson

Courtesy of the Paul Hennefeld Gay and Lesbian History On Stamps Collection

150

FIGHT AIDS WORLDWIDE

LUTTE MONDIALE CONTRE LE SIDA

FIRST DAY OF ISSUE · WFUNA CACHET

WORLD FEDERATION OF
UNITED NATIONS ASSOCIATIONS

*Official
First Day
of Issue*

MOBY DICK

Saluting
Herman Melville
NOVELIST · POET
LITERARY ARTS SERIES · 1984

151

SEX DEVOLUTION: SEXUAL IDEOLOGY ON THE ORIGIN OF WOMEN'S OPPRESSIONS   *excerpt and chart from LESBIAN ORIGINS by Susan Cavin, Ph.D.*

There is a logic to the ideology of sex. I use a critical method that is as simple as a coin toss to demystify sexual ideology. I divide society, history, sexuality or any other social phenomenon into two coins, a female and a male coin. Each coin has two sides, heads and tails. Heads is always the female version of the social phenomenon. Tails is always the male version of the same phenomenon. This is a lesbian feminist method!

...Hystory has several meanings. Hystory refers in one sense to the time of prehistory, pre-patriarchy, pre-recorded time; while history denotes the time of patriarchy and written records. Hystory is also the story of women as told by "women-identified-women" (herstory), while history is the story of men as told by male-identified males." History is distinctly male as hystory is distinctly female, ideologically.

...According to these lesbian feminist usages, objectively neutral history does not exist. Instead, the recording or retelling of past events depends upon the sex, race, class, age, sexual preference, religion, politics and other relevant sociological identifications of the observer. Thus, it is impossible to remove the observer...from the observation.

Paradigm of Sexual Ideology as a Coin Toss		
COIN TOSS	**SEXUAL IDEOLOGY**	
Socio-Sexual Events: 2 Coins	**Tails=** **Male Ideology**	**Heads=** **Female Ideology**
Male Event= Male Coin (history)	1) capitalist patriarchists *(male version of history)*	2) hetero-feminists bourgeois feminists *(female version of male history)*
Female Event= Female Coin (hystory)	3) male matriarchists & marxists *(male version of hystory)*	4) lesbian feminists & lesbian separatists *(female version of hystory)*

LESBIAN ORIGINS, by Susan Cavin (c) 1985 by Susan Cavin ISM PRESS

152

TEXTBOOKS: PROVIDING FAIR INFORMATION

by Jessea Greenman

...For society as a whole, greater knowledge of the valuable roles that lesbian, gay, and bisexual people have always played would overcome the erroneous stereotypes most people have about our community. This would enable society to more fully utilize the talents and energies of our people. Furthermore, such information is needed if people are to have an accurate understanding of world history and literature. It can be argued, for example, that Alexander the Great ended his drive for expanded empire because his male lover died, leaving Alexander too bereft to continue his conquests. It can be argued that Eleanor Roosevelt intended that the UN International Declaration of Human Rights, of which she is the chief architect, be interpreted to protect lesbian, gay and bisexual people (contrary to the current spurious interpretation) because not only were some of her best friends lesbian but she herself loved another woman. We cannot begin to analyze correctly the works of Whitman, Baldwin, Woolf, Garcia Lorca, Hansberry, Mishima, Dickinson or myriads of others unless we appreciate their lesbian, gay, and bisexual sensibilities.

❖❖❖❖❖❖❖❖❖❖❖❖❖❖❖❖❖❖❖❖❖❖❖❖❖❖❖❖❖❖❖❖❖❖❖❖

From a statement made by Jessea Greenman, GLAAD, San Francisco Bay Area Chapter, in a communication titled: Public Schools' Duty: Providing Fair Information on Sexual Orientation. She participates in several efforts to obtain inclusion throughout the nation.

❖❖❖❖❖❖❖❖❖❖❖❖❖❖❖❖❖❖❖❖❖❖❖❖❖❖❖❖❖❖❖❖❖❖❖❖

WRITING WORD PROBLEMS THAT REFLECT CULTURAL DIVERSITY   by John Kellermeier

Portions of this article appeared in TRANSFORMATIONS, The New Jersey Project Journal, editor Sylvia K.Baer, Ph.D., Gloucester County College

I teach an introductory statistics course. To illustrate a particular concept in probability, I can use a word problem such as the following:

An urn contains four red balls and six green balls. A ball is drawn from this urn and its color recorded. The ball is then replaced. This is repeated for a total of ten draws. How many of these balls would you expect to be red?

The overt curriculum is the method for determining expected counts. The hidden curriculum is about urns and balls, a not very interesting topic at that. On the other hand, I can teach the same overt curriculum with the following problem:

In sixty-five percent of all rapes, the victim knows her assailant. If we interview twenty women who were raped, what is the probability that no more than four of them were raped by strangers?

In many of our courses, we use word problems, case studies, and examples to teach and to illustrate our subject matter. All of these applications have an overt curriculum and a hidden curriculum. The overt curriculum is the subject matter we are trying to teach, while the hidden curriculum is the content of the applications.

In this case, the overt curriculum is still the fact that acquaintance rape accounts for sixty-five percent of all rape.

This is an example of how this hidden curriculum can be used to reflect cultural diversity and to incorporate issues of race, class, and gender, particularly in those subject areas where such issues seem to have no relevance.

Why do we want to do this?

1. We live in a society in which diversity is used to marginalize people, a society in which power and privilege are based on a "norm" or standard of rightness. To balance this, there is a need to celebrate and expand acceptence of diverse peoples and cultures. This is important for those people who are in the "normative" groups as well as for those who are marginalized.

2. Students learn more easily when the subject matter is related to their lives. Students, praticularly those marginalized by race, class, gender, sexual orientation, etc., are more willing and able to engage the overt curriculum if they can understand and see themselves in the hidden curriculum.

3. The demographics of North American society are changing, reflecting an increasingly diverse population. Additionally, global society is becoming increasingly interconnected through economic and informational networks. It is becoming more important for our students to appreciate and begin to value cultural diversity if they are to function as global citizens.

4. The inclusion of issues of race, class, and gender breaks down the image of areas such as math and science as white-male domains. This, in turn, serves to give increased access to these areas to students who have been marginalized by the traditional images...

USING DIVERSITY AS BACKGROUND

The first type of word problem I will illustrate uses issues of diversity as a background. The first of these two problems uses women's literature and the second uses names from diverse cultures as settings for questions about probability and statistics topics.

- An assignment for a literature course is to read five short stories by women: "Elethia" by Alice Walker, "Seventeen Syllables" by Hisaye Yamamoto, "Recuerdo" by Guadalupe Valdes Fallis, "Storyteller" by Leslie Marmon Silko, and "Only a Phase" by Leslea Newman. The students will then be asked in class to write essays on three of the five stories randomly chosen by the instructor. Suppose a student only reads "Elethia," "Recuerdo," and "Storyteller." Consider the following events:

A. The student has read at least of the stories selected.

B. The stories by Alice Walker and Leslea Newman are among those selected for essays.

a. What type of sampling is used in this situation?

b. List the samples in the sample space.

c. List the samples in each of the events A and B.

d. What are the probabilities of each of the events of A and B?

- *John and David kept records of their food cost for a sample of 9 days when they were on vacation. Their mean cost was $30.75 with a standard deviation of $7.65. Calculate a 95% confidence interval for the average amount of money this couple spends on food per day while on vacation.*

- *An assignment for a gay studies course is to choose two of the following books to read and write a report on.*

ANOTHER MOTHER TONGUE: GAY WORDS, GAY WORLDS
      by Judy Grahn
THE PINK TRIANGLE: THE NAZI WAR AGAINST HOMOSEXUALS
      by Richard Plant
GAY SPIRIT: MYTH AND MEANING edited by Mark Thompson
IN THE LIFE: A BLACK GAY ANTHOLOGY edited by Joseph Beam
LIVING THE SPIRIT: A GAY AMERICAN INDIAN ANTHOLOGY
      edited by Will Roscoe

Suppose a student in this course decided to pick the books randomly. Consider the following events:

    A: At least one book chosen is an edited anthology.
    B: At least one book chosen is about people of color.

a. *What type of sampling is used in this situation?*
b. *List the samples in the sample space.*
c. *List the samples in each of the events A and B.*
d. *What are the probabilities of each of the events A and B.*

- *A sample of eight students was given a test designed to measure how much they knew about AIDS and HIV. Their names and scores were:*

Name	Score
Haji	92
George	88
Susan	91
Consuela	83
Rashida	86
Sola	84
Kyoko	92
Joshua	75

a. *Find the mean and median of this sample.*
b. *Find the range of this sample.*
c. *Find the variance and standard deviation of this sample.*

156

USING FACTS ABOUT DIVERSE POPULATIONS

The following problems use statistical information about diverse populations and issues of race, class, gender, and sexual orientation as a basis for asking probability and statistics questions. The information presented in these problems is gleaned from a variety of sources such as journal and newspaper articles and women's studies textbooks.

- The annual incomes of African-American single mothers in a large metropolitan population area have a mean of $5,260 and a standard deviation of $2,040. If 100 such women are sampled, what is the probability that their average annual income will be above $5,500?

- Today, only about 10 percent of American families fit the traditional model of the nuclear family - a married, heterosexual couple with the husband the only wage earner. Suppose a sample of twenty American families is selected.

a. How many of these families would you expect to fit the traditional model?

b. What is the probability that at least four of these families fit the traditional model?

c. What is the probability that two or more of these families DO NOT fit the traditional model?

A lesbian comes out to herself and the world after leaving college. As she becomes acquainted with the gay community in her city she meets 5 former college classmates all of whom are gay. Studies of gay men and lesbians who attended her college show that 38% concealed their sexual orientation while in school.

a. How likely is it that all of these former classmates were out in college?

b. How many of these former classmates should she expect to have been in the closet while in college.

c. How likely is it that at least one of these former classmates were out in college?

2. A recent study shows that 80% of people who identify as lesbian, bisexual or gay have experienced some kind of harassment or violence because of their sexual orientation. Suppose a reporter samples twenty bisexuals, gays and lesbians at a Gay Pride march. What is the probability that at least 15 of them would have experienced some such harassment or violence?

157

USING REALISTIC DATA ABOUT DIVERSE POPULATIONS

   This next group of problems also uses facts or information about diverse populations. In these problems, however, the information is uncovered by the process of doing the problem. The sample data given in these problems are not "real data" in the sense that they are not taken from actual studies. Rather, they are "realistic data" simulated on the basis of the results of actual studies.

   - In a study of slavery in America, the histories of forty recorded slave marriages were studied to determine if they remained intact or were disrupted. The causes of disruptions of these marriages were determined to be the sale of a spouse, the death of a spouse, or the choice of the married couple. These were coded as Sale, Death, and Choice, respectively. In some of the marriages, there was no disruption, which was then coded as None. The results were:

Sale	None	Death	Sale	Death	Sale	None	Sale	Death	Sale
Choice	Death	Death	Sale	None	Sale	Death	Death	Sale	Death
Death	Death	Death	Sale	Choice	Death	Sale	None	Death	None
Sale	Choice	Sale	Death	Death	Choice	Death	Sale	Death	Death

Organize these data into a table and draw a bargraph.

   - *A random sample of college faculty were asked their gender (coded as M for male and F for female) and their faculty rank (coded as INS for instructor, AST for assistant professor, ASO for associate professor, and FPR for full professor). The results:*

M ASO	M AST	M ASO	M ASO	M AST
M AST	M FPR	M INS	F ASO	F AST
M AST	F FPR	M AST	M ASO	M AST
M FPR	M AST	M INS	M FPR	M AST
M INS	M ASO	M FPR	F AST	F AST
M AST	M AST	M ASO	F INS	M AST
M ASO	M ASO	F INS	F AST	M INS
M AST	M ASO	M ASO	M AST	F ASO
M ASO	F AST	F INS	M ASO	M AST
M AST	F AST	M ASO	M AST	F INS

   a. *Organize these data in a contingency table.*
   b. *Determine the cell proportions for gender classes.*
   c. *Draw a bargraph for these data.*

158

USING FACTS THAT MAKE A POINT ABOUT DIVERSE POPULATIONS

In a sample of 133 lesbians, gay men and bisexuals, 59 reported they had encountered some type of employment discrimination because of their sexual orientation. Determine a 95% confidence interval for the percentage of lesbians, gay men and bisexuals who encounter employment discrimination.

From working this problem students learn that 44% of lesbigays experience employment discrimination based on their sexual orientation.

Gay men, bisexuals and lesbians who experience violence against them because of their sexual orientation sometimes face a further problem if they choose to report the incident to the police, namely that the police themselves may be discouraging in the persuit of the matter. To study this, 50 lesbigay people who had reported such violence to police were asked whether the attitudes of the police had been encouraging, discouraging or neutral.
Organize these data in a table and draw a bargraph:

Neutral	Discouraging	Discouraging	Discouraging
Neutral	Discouraging	Encouraging	Neutral
Neutral	Neutral	Discouraging	Encouraging
Encouraging	Discouraging	Neutral	Discouraging
Neutral	Encouraging	Neutral	Discouraging
Neutral	Discouraging	Neutral	Discouraging
Neutral	Discouraging	Discouraging	Discouraging
Neutral	Encouraging	Encouraging	Neutral
Neutral	Discouraging	Discouraging	Discouraging
Discouraging	Neutral	Discouraging	Neutral
Neutral	Discouraging	Neutral	Discouraging
Neutral	Neutral	Neutral	Discouraging
Encouraging	Neutral		

❖❖❖

John Kellermeier ❖ *A 43 year-old Associate Professor of Mathematics at SUNY, Plattsburgh. He has been teaching statistics for thirteen years and women's studies for three years. His research interests are in gender issues in mathematics and in feminist pedagogy in the mathematics and statistics classroom. He is currently writing a textbook, JOY OF STATISTICS, for an elementary statistics course which incorporates issues of cultural diversity into word problems. He is a faculty advisor to the Lesbian Gay Bisexual Alliance and to Men Confronting Sexism.*

❖❖❖

READING LIST FOR GAY AND LESBIAN LITERATURE   prepared by B.V. Marshall

Below is a list of works which may be considered for the course in
Gay and Lesbian Literature. The works have received serious
critical notice and study in regard to their literary content and,
in particular, in regards to homosexuality in a literary context.

1. Anthologies

   Beam, Joseph editor In the Life: A Black Gay Anthology.
   Boston: Alyson Publications,. 1986.

   Coote, Stephen editor The Penguin Book of Homosexual Verse.
   Harmondsworth, England: Penguin Books, 1986.

   Decarnin, Camilla, Eric Garber, and Lyn Paleo editors Worlds
   Apart: An Anthology of Lesbian and Gay Science Fiction and
   Fantasy. Boston: Alyson Publications, 1986

   Hadas, Rachael - Unending Dialogue: Voices from an AIDS
   Poetry Workshop. Boston: Faber and Faber, 1991.

   Hemphill, Essex and Joseph Beam editors. Brother to Brother
   New Writing by Black Gay Men. Boston: Alyson Publications
   1991.

   Jurrist, Charles editor Shadows of Love: Gay American Fiction
   Boston: Alyson Publications, 1988.

   Klein, Michael editor Poets for Life, Seventy-Six Poets
   Respond to AIDS. New York: Crown Publishers, 1989.

   Morse, Carl and Joan Larkin editors. Gay and Lesbian Poetry
   in Our Time. New York: St. Martin's Press, 1988.

   Osborn, M. Elizabeth, editor The Way We Live Now: American
   Plays and the AIDS Crisis. New York: Theatre Communications
   Group, Inc. 1990.

   Shewey, Don editor, Out Front, Contemporary Gay and Lesbian
   Plays. Grove Press: New York, 1988.

   White, Edmund, editor The Faber Book of Gay Short Fiction.
   London and Boston: Faber and Faber, 1991.

160

2. Literature <u>and</u> <u>Authors</u> <u>Prior</u> <u>to</u> <u>1945</u>

Many of the poets listed can be found in the Penguin book of Homosexual verse (listed above).

Sappho	Catullus	Meleager	Strato
Martial	Paul Verlaine	Arthur Rimbaud	C.P. Cavafy
Walt Whitman	A.E. Housman	Oscar Wilde	Renee Vivian
Gertrude Stein			

<u>Fiction</u> <u>and</u> <u>Creative</u> <u>Non-Fiction</u>

Forster, E.M.	<u>Maurice</u>
Genet, Jean	<u>Our</u> <u>Lady</u> <u>of</u> <u>the</u> <u>Flowers</u>
Gide, Andre.	<u>The</u> <u>Immoralist</u>
Hall, Radclyffe	<u>The</u> <u>Well</u> <u>of</u> <u>Loneliness</u>
Isherwood, Christopher	<u>Berlin</u> <u>Stories</u>, <u>Christopher</u> <u>and</u> <u>His</u> <u>Kind</u>, <u>A</u> <u>Single</u> <u>Man</u>
James, Henry	<u>The</u> <u>Pupil</u>
Melville, Herman	<u>Billy</u> <u>Budd</u>
Stein, Gertrude	<u>The</u> <u>Autobiography</u> <u>of</u> <u>Alice</u> <u>B.</u> <u>Toklas</u>
Wilde, Oscar	<u>Portrait</u> <u>of</u> <u>Dorian</u> <u>Gray</u>
Woolf, Virginia	<u>Orlando</u>

3. <u>Literature</u> <u>after</u> <u>1945</u>

<u>Fiction</u>

Allison, Dorothy	<u>Trash</u>
	<u>Bastard</u> <u>Out</u> <u>of</u> <u>Carolina</u>
Baldwin, James	<u>Another</u> <u>Country</u>
	<u>Giovanni's</u> <u>Room</u>
	<u>Just</u> <u>Above</u> <u>My</u> <u>Head</u>
Brown, Rita Mae	<u>Rubyfruit</u> <u>Jungle</u>
Burroughs, William	<u>Naked</u> <u>Lunch</u>
Capote, Truman	<u>Other</u> <u>Voices</u>, <u>Other</u> <u>Rooms</u>
Cunningham, Michael	<u>A</u> <u>Home</u> <u>at</u> <u>the</u> <u>End</u> <u>of</u> <u>the</u> <u>World</u>
Dixon, Melvin	<u>Vanishing</u> <u>Rooms</u>

Fienberg, David	Eighty-Sixed
	Spontaneous Combustion
Flagg, Fannie	Fried Green Tomatoes at the Whistle Stop Cafe
Gomez, Jewelle	The Gilda Stories
Hansen, Joseph	A Country of Old Men
Leavitt, David	Family Dancing
	The Lost Language of Cranes
Rechy, John	City of Night
Tsui, Kitty	The Words of A Woman Who Breathes Fire
Vidal, Gore	The City and The Pillar
Walker, Alice	The Color Purple
White, Edmund	A Boy's Own Story
	Forgetting Elena
ed.	The Faber Book of Gay Short Fiction

Poetry by:

John Ashberry	Elizabeth Bishop	Olga Broumas
Robert Duncan	Allen Ginsberg	Robert Gluck
Jewelle Gomez	Thom Gunn	Marilyn Hacker
Joy Harjo	June Jordan	Audre Lorde
James Merrill	Frank O'Hara	Muriel Rukeyser

Minnie Bruce Pratt - Crimes Against Nature
Adrienne Rich - 21 Love Poems

Drama

Fierstein, Harvey	Torch Song Trilogy, On Tidy Endings
Hellman, Lillian	The Children's Hour
Hoffman, William	As Is
Kondoleon, Harry	Zero Positive
Kushner, Tony	Angels in America

162

Kramer, Larry	The Normal Heart
Lucas, Craig	Blue Window
Ludlam, Charles	Camille Collected Plays
Mann, Emily	The Execution of Justice
Orton, Joe	Loot What the Butler Saw Prick Up Your Ears
Parnell, Peter	Romance Language
Sherman, Martin	Bent
Williams, Tennesse	Cat on a Hot Tin Roof

4. Non-Fiction

Many of the following selections should be considered as supplementary resources.

A. Autobiography/Biography

Clarke, Gerald	Capote, New York: Simon and Schuster, 1988.
Duberman, Martin	Cures: A Gay Man's Odyssey. New York: Dutton, 1991.
Lahr, John	Prick Up Your Ears New York: Limelight, 1986
Lorde, Audre	Zami, A New Spelling of My Name, Biomythography, Trumansburg, New York: The Crossing Press, 1983.
	The Cancer Journals San Francisco: Aunt Lute Books, 1980.
Monette, Paul	Borrowed Time New York: Harcourt, Brace Jovanovich, 1988.
	Becoming a Man New York: Harcourt, Brace Jovanovich, 1992

Preston, John, Editor, <u>Hometowns: Gay Men Write About Where They Belong,</u> Penguin Books USA: Dutton, 1991

Shilts, Randy   <u>The Mayor of Castro Street</u> New York: St. Martin Press, 1983

Wojnarowicz, David   <u>Close to the Knives</u> New York: Vintage Books , 1991.

B.   History and Sociology

Boswell, John   <u>Christianity, Social Tolerance and Homosexuality</u> Chicago: University of Chicago Press, 1981.

Cowan Thomas   <u>Gay Men and Women Who Enriched The World.</u> Boston: Alyson Publications, 1988.

D'Emilio, John   <u>Sexual Politics, Sexual Communities: The Making of a Homosexual Minority in the United States 1940-1970</u> Chicago: Univerisyt of Chicago Press, 1983.

Duberman, Martin Bauml Martha Vicinus and George Chancey, Jr.   <u>Hidden From History: Reclaiming the Gay and Lesbian Past,</u> New York: New American Library, Penguin Books, Inc. New York, Marrham, Ontario, 1989.

Holleran, Andrew   <u>Ground Zero,</u> New York: New American Library, 1989

Jay, Karla, and Allen Young,   <u>Out of the Closet: Voices of Gay Liberation.</u> New York: New York University Press, New York and London 1972. Revised 1992.

Katz, Jonathan Editor,   <u>Gay American History: Lesbians and Gay Men in the U. S. A.</u> New York: Thomas Crowell, 1976.

Miller, Neil   <u>In Search of Gay America: Women and Men in a Time of Change.</u> Boston: Atlantic Monthly Press. 1989

Roscoe, Will Coordinating Editor <u>Living the Spirit,</u> a Gay

164

American Indian Anthology. New York:
St. Martin's Press, 1988.

Shilts, Randy   And the Band Played On. New York: St.
                    Martin's Press, 1987.

Williams, Walter L. The Spirit and The Flesh: Sexual
                     Diversity in American Indian Culture
                     Boston: Beacon Press, 1986.

C. Aesthetics

Cooper, Emmanuel   The Sexual Perspective: Homosexuality
                    and Art in the Last 100 Years in the
                    West. London and New York: Routledge
                    and Kegan Paul, 1989.
Kalstone, David   Five Temperments Boston: Norton,
                    Date not established.

Sontag, Susan   Notes on Camp found in A Susan Sontag
                    Reader New York: Farrar Strauss and
                    Giroux, 1982.
                    Illness as Metaphor New York: Farrar,
                    Straus & Giroux, 1997
                    AIDS and Its Metaphors New York: Farrar
                    Strauss and Giroux, 1989.

Russo, Vito   The Celluloid Closet, Rev. 1987, Harper
                    and Row, NY.

D. Books For Children

Brown, Forman   The Generous Jefferson Bartleby Jones
                    Boston: Alyson 1991.

Elwin, Rosamund   Asha's Mums Boston: Alyson, 1990

Newman, Leslea   Belinda's Bouquet Boston: Alyson, 1991.
                    Gloria Goes to Gay Pride Boston: Alyson
                    1991.
                    Heather Has Two Mommies, Boston: Alyson
                    1991.

Severance, Jane   When Megan Went Away Carboro, North
                    Carolina: Lollipop Power Press, 1983.

Valentine, Johnny   The Daddy Machine Boston: Alyson,
                    1991

                    The Duke Who Outlawed Jelly Beans and
                    Other Stories Boston: Alyson 1991

Willhoite, Michael   Daddy's Roommate Boston: Alyson 1990
                     The Entertainer Boston: Alyson 1991
                     Families: A Coloring Book Boston:
                     Alyson 1991

B.V. Marshall ❖ *Holds an M.F.A. in creative writing from the University of Massachusetts in Amherst. Having lived and taught in Libya, Jordan and Kuwait, he currently teaches in the English Department at Middlesex County College in New Jersey. A playwright as well as a poet, he has produced plays around the country. He was awarded a fellowship from the National Endowment for the Humanities for study of African-American in the Performing Arts, and twice awarded fellowships from the New Jersey State Council on the Arts for playwriting.*

Courtesy of the Paul Hennefeld Gay and Lesbian History on Stamps Collection

A
BIBLIOGRAPHY

From the Archives of
THE TEACHERS' GROUP
Gays and Lesbians working in education

GAY AND LESBIAN ISSUES IN EDUCATION

Mr. Tracy Phariss

Featuring Lesbian/Gay
Individuals or Issues

And God Loves Each One. Ann Thompson Cook, Dumbarton United Methodist
Church Task Force on Reconciliation, P.O. Box 23636, Washington, DC
20026. (1987) $4.95. (grades 6-10). Excellent book that deals specifically with
gay/lesbian youth.

Asha's Mums. Rosamund Elwin and Michele Paulse, Women's Press, 517 College
Street, Suite 233, Toronto, Ontario, Canada M6G 4A2. (1990). $5.95, pp. 24.
(grades k-5). Asha, her teacher, and her two moms help other students understand their loving family. The main characters are African-American. *

Asking About Sex and Growing Up. Joanna Cole, Morrow. (1988). $12.95, pp. 128.
(grades 4-6). Topics include homosexuality, crushes, sex etc.

Coping With...Your Sexual Orientation. Deborah A. Miller and Alex Waigandt, New
York: Rosen Publishing Group. (1990). $13.95, pp. 104. (school library). An
excellent library book in the 22 book series "Coping With ..." Especially designed for the public school system.

Daddy Machine, The. Jonny Valentine, Boston: Alyson Publication. (1991). $6.95.
(grades k-4). The story of two sisters who live with their two lesbian mothers.
One day they fantasize about having a father - they get their wish and more.

Daddy's Roommate. Michael Willhoite, Boston: Alyson Publications. (1990) $6.95,
pp. 30. (grades k - 4). An excellent story book that deals with the divorce and
the loving relationship of a young boy's father. A young boy's father and his
father's lover take part in activities familiar to all kinds of families: cleaning
the house, shopping, playing games, fighting and making up. *

Duke Who Outlawed Jelly Beans and Other Stories, The. Jonny Valentine, Boston:
Alyson. (1991). $12.95. (grades 3-6). A delightful collection looking at diversi-
ty issues. *

Families: A Celebration of Diversity, Commitment and Love. Aylette Jenness, New
York: Houghton Mifflin. (1990). (grades k-6). Interracial, single-parent,
communal, extended and foster families are included along with 2 households
with gay/lesbian members. A super addition. *

Families: a coloring book. Michael Willhoite, Boston: Alyson Pub. (1991) $2.95,
pp. 32. (grade k-5). A coloring book about families including gay/lesbian families. *

Generous Jefferson Bartleby Jones,The. Forman Brown, Boston: Alyson Pub. (1991).
pp. 38, $7.95. (grades k-4). A boy with two dads finds that one of them is always
free to have fun with until he loans them out, to generously. *

Gloria Goes to Gay Pride. Leslea Newman, Boston: Alyson Pub. (1991). $7.95, pp. 34.
(grades k-4). Describes, from the viewpoint of a young girl, just what makes up
Gay Pride Day a fun, special day for Gloria and her two mothers.

Heather Has Two Mommies. Leslea Newman and Diana Souza, In Other Words
Publishers, 351 Pleasant Street, Suite 233, Northampton, MA 01060. (1989).
$6.95, pp. 22. (grades k-4). Explains to children the loving relationship of
Lesbian mothers. Three-year-old Heather discovers other students have dad-
dies, but her confusion is dispelled by an adult instructor. *

How Babies and Families are Made (There is more than one way!). Patricia Schaffer,
Tabor Sarah (415-843-2779). (1988). (grades k-4). Families can be created by
many different ways including insemination and adoption. This book also
includes basic information on C-sections, miscarriage, premature birth, and
babies born differently abled.

How Would You Feel If Your Dad Was Gay?. Ann Heron and Meredith Maran, Boston: Alyson Pub. (1991). $9.95, pp. 33. (grade 3-6). Jasmine and her brother disagree about telling others of their gay father. Provides role models for children in these nontraditional families and to give insight into the unique problems they face. The main characters are African-American.

In The Tent. David Rees, Boston: Alyson Pub. (1983). $2.25, pp. 208. (grades 5-6 - good readers). Growing up Catholic and Gay. Mild, deals with only feelings.

Jenny Lives With Eric and Martin. Susanne Bosche, Boston: Alyson Pub. (1983). $5.50, pp. 52. (grades k-6). Examines the life of Jenny, a 6 yr old girl, who lives with her father and his lover. Handles a brief scene with a homophobic neighbor very well.

Kid's Book of Divorce: By, For, and About Kids. Eric E. Rofes, Fayerweather Street School. (1981). $3.95, pp. 112. (grades k-6). Section titled "Loving Your Gay Parent."

Learning About Sex - A Contemporary Guide for Young Adults. Gary F. Kelly, New York: Barron's Educational Series, Inc, (1987). $3.50, pp. 189. (grades 5-6). For use in middle school sex education classes. *

Lots of Mommies. Jane Servance, Lollipop Power, P.O. Box 1171 Chapel Hill, NC 27514. (1983). $5.00, (grades k - 3). An unusual account of child living in a womyn's collective.

Milkman's On His Way..., The. David Rees, Boston: Alyson Press, USA. (1982). $7.95, pp. 118. (grades 5-6 - good readers). A young boy grows up gay with accepting friends.

Truth About Alex, The. Anne Snyder and Louis Pelletier, (original title: Counter Play; New York: A Signet Book/New American Library. (1981). $2.75, pp. 166. (advanced 5th - 9). As seen on the HBO special of the same title. High School student's friendship is explored. Peer/parent pressure and coming out are the main themes.

Understanding Sexual Identity: A Book for Gay Teens and Their Friends. Janice E. Rench, Minneapolis: Lerner Publications Company. (1990). pp. 59. (school library). An excellent book for the school library, printed with reinforced binding. This book will not try to determine a child's sexual orientation, but will dispel some of the myths about gays and lesbians and help readers better understand their own sexuality. Nongay readers will learn how to be more supportive of their gay friends, and gay readers will learn that they are not alone.

What Happened to Mr. Forster?. Gary Bargar, New York: Claion/Houghton Mifflin. 1981, pp. 169. (grades 4-7). A gay teacher helps a 6th grade student gain self-esteem.

When Megan Went Away. Jane Servance, Lollipop Power, P.O. Box 1171 Chapel Hill, NC 27514. (1979). $4.00, pp. 32. (grades 1-5). Deals with lesbian mothers divorce. One of the first picture books to deal with gay/lesbian families.

Your Family, My Family. Joan Drescher. Meredith Tax, Walker & Co. (1981). $7.95, pp. 32. (grades 1-5). A picture book about families including gay families.

Relating to HIV/AIDS

AIDS: A Primer for Children. Janice Koch, Berret Publications, Roslyn, NY, 1-516-365-4040. (grades 3-6). Provides factual information and encourages students to ask questions. Includes a guide for parents or teachers. Spanish edition available.

Children and the AIDS Virus. Rosiemarie Hausherr, Clarion: Kinderbooks, Johnsbury, VT, 1-802-748-4371. (1989) (grades k-6). A read-aloud text with true stories, that describes the immune system and the virus that causes AIDS.

Let's Talk About AIDS. Channing L. Bette Company. South Deerfield, MA, 1-800-828-2827. (grades 4-8). Five pages of information and activities for children.

Let's Talk About Sex. Sam Gitchel, Network Publications, Santa Cruz , CA, 1-800-321-4407. (grades 3-7). This book is a read and discuss guide for children and their parents. Available in Spanish.

Losing Uncle Tim. Mary Kate Jordan, Morton Grove, IL 1-800-255-7675. (1989). (grades k-4). A simple yet realistic account of a young boys acceptance that his Uncle's Tim has AIDS. Uncle Tim's prolonged illness and eventual death is handle very well. *

My Name is Jonathan (and I have AIDS). Sharon Schilling, Prickly Pair. (1990). (grades 3-6). Candid first person photo essay. Provides an intimate, in-depth view of Jonathan's life - having lived with HIV since birth.

Risky Times. Jeanne Blake, New York: Workman Publishing. (1990) $5.95, pp. 158. (6th grade sex ed class). Explores the issue of AIDS, discussing such aspects as sex, condom use, peer pressure, drug use, and decision making.

Z' Gift. Neal Starkman, Comprehensive Health Education Foundation, Seattle, WA, 1-206-824-2907. (grades 3-6). A young boy responds to the news that his teacher has AIDS, and then teaches adults the meaning of compassion.

Self-esteem

An Enchanted Hair Tale. Alexis DeVeaux, Harper and Row. (1987). (grades 1-3). Sudan's is teased by his peers because of his flowing hair. Sudan leaves home and find a group of people with similar flowing hair who appreciate him.

Delphine. Molly Bang, Marrow. (1988). Delphine make a perilous journey with a wolf and a cougar across mountains and raging rivers.

Frog and Toad are Friends. Arnold Lobel, Harper and Row. (1970). (grades k-3). A classic story where true friendship between males is achieved.

Jesse's Dream Skirt. Bruce Mack, Lollipop Power. (1979). (grades k-4). Jess, who loves to wrap himself in sheets, dreams of wearing a multicolored skirt. His mother makes it for him. A understanding daycare teachers leads the children in a discussion that enables them to reevaluate notions about gender roles.

Man Whose Mother Was a Pirate, The. Margaret Mahy, Viking. (1986). (grades 1-4). A mother and her son take a trip to the sea. The son's life is greatly influenced by his mother, a former pirate.

Oliver Button is a Sissy. Tomi DePaola, Harcourt, Brace, Jovanovich. (1979). (grades k-4). A young boys doesn't give into peer pressure.

What is a Girl? What is a Boy?. Stephanie Waxman, Thomas Y. Crowell. (1989). (grades k-3). It uses B&W photographs to break down sex role stereotypes. Boys and girls are shown in a variety of nontraditional activities. *

William's Doll. Charlie Zoltow, Harper and Row. (1972). (grades k-2). William is a little boy who wants a doll to hug and cuddle. William's father doesn't think boys should have dolls. William's grandmother supports William's need for the baby doll.

170

Biographies

Beautiful Room is Empty, The. Edmund White, Ballantine Book. (1988). $4.95, pp. 199, 8-12. Semi-autobiographical of his life from the 1950-1960.

Best Little Boy in the World, The. John Reid, New York: Ballantine. (1976). $3.75, pp. 213, 9-12. Excellent, basically autobiographical.

Black Lesbian in White America. Anita Cornwell, Naiad Press. (1983). $7.50, pp. 144, 8-12. Retrospective of a black lesbian feminist. **

Confessions of a Mask. Ykio Mishima, A New Directions Paperback. (1958). $4.95, pp. 253, 10-12. Reprinted - 1988. Details growing up gay in postwar Japan.

David Kopay Story, The. David Kopay, Primus, Donald I. Fine Inc., 128 East 36th Street, New York, NY 10016. (1978). $8.95, pp. 279, 7-12. Republished - 1988 with new material. A ten year veteran gay football star's personal story. ***

Mayor of Castro Street. Randy Shilts, St Martins' Press. $10.95. Biography of Harvey Milk, the noted gay politician.

Reflections of a Rock Lobster: A Story About Growing Up Gay. Aaron Ficke, Boston: Alyson Pub., Carrier Pigeon. (1981). $5.95, pp. 120, 7-12. A young gay man talks openly about his life and a legal battle to take another male and not a female to the High School Prom. ** ***

Rubyfruit Jungle. Rita Mae Brown, Bantam. (1977). $3.95, pp. 217, 9-12. Semi-autobiographical from working class women growing up lesbian. ***

Sudden Strangers. Aaron and Walter Ficke, St. Martin's Press. Aaron Ficke and his father discuss how their relationship changed.

Yesterday's Lessons. Sharon Isabell, Oakland, CA: Women's Press. (1974). A young women growing up out-of-the-closet in the 1940's and 50's.

Fiction

A Boy's Own Story. Edmund White, Ballantine Book. (1986). $4.95, pp. 190, 7-12. An excellent story of a boy growing up.

All-American Boy. Frank Nosca, Boston: Alyson. (1983). pp. 166, 7-12. 17 year old tells his story of his love with Paul. Homophobic classmate, melodrama of first love, fag-bashing but has a happy ending.

Arizona Kid, The. Ron Koertge, Boston: Joy Street/Little, Brown. (1988). pp. 228, 7-12. Over a summer, a 16 year old boy gets to understand his gay uncle while telling a story of a gay community. **

Annie on my Mind. Nancy Garden, Farrar, Status & Giroux. (1982). $11.95, pp. 350, 7-12. The magic of first love between Liza and Annie is looked at. ***

Bad Boy. Diana Wieler, Delacorte Press. (1989). $15.00, pp. 184. 7-12. An honest look at teenage sexuality and the world of high school hockey. The realistic rage one team member has toward his best friend and teammate who is gay is amazing. ***

Boys on the Rock, The. John Fox, Plume Books. (1984).

Changelings. Jo Sinclair, Feminist Press. $8.95. Two teenage girls, one Jewish, one black build a loving friendship despite racial strife form neighbors.

Chronicles of Tornor. Elizabeth Lynn, Berkeley Books. (1978-1980). (NIP). A trilogy of a mystical society where there is no homophobia.

Common Sons. Ronald E. Doaghe, Austin, Tx.: Banned Books. (1989). $8.95. Well written book about two young teens who deal with friendship and love, a few sex scenes are realistically described.

Course of True Love Never Did Run Smooth, The. Marilyn Singer, New York: Harper and Row. (1983). pp. 246. Tells a story of high school students falling in love, gay and straight love.

Counter Play. Anne Snyder. (1983). $2.25, pp. 176, 7-12. Concerns a friend standing by his gay friend. Rename to The Truth About Alex, and an HBO video.

Crush. Jane Futcher, Boston: Alyson Pub. (1988). $7.95. pp. 255. 9-12. A wonderful high school lesbian romance, rich with developing sexuality and attraction - very true with the pain and joys of adolescent love. ***

Drowning of Stephan Jones, The. Bette Greene, New York: Bantam Books. (1991). $16.00, pp. 218. 9-12. A young man's homophobia ultimately leads to a night of murderous violence. The cause of justice and the quest against oppression is championed with a great deal of work. ***

Enchanted Boy. Richie McMullen, GMP Publisher Ltd., P.O. Box 247, London N1790r. (1989). 11-12. deals with sexual abuse as a child, prostitution. First book in a series, relates a story a a boy growing up, age 5-15. The second in the series is Enchanted Youth (1990). Deals with this young boy growing up to be a professional youth counselor/worker in London.

Front Runner, The. Patricia Warren, New York: William Morrow and Company. (1974). $7.95, pp. 324, 9-12. A gay male athlete in college deals with his love.

Happy Ending Are All Alike. Sandra Scoppettone, Harper & Row. (1978). $11.89, pp. 202, 7-12. Two girls confront and surmount being lesbians in High School.

Hey, Dollface. Deborah Hautzig, Greenwillow Books. (1978). $11.88, pp. 151, (NIP), 7-9. Val and Chloe growing up in New York. **

Homosexual As Hero in Contemporary Fiction, The. Stephen Adams, (Critical Studies Series), B & N Imports. (1980). $28.50, pp. 208.

Horizon of the Heart. Shelly Smith, The Naiad Press Inc., P.O. Box 10543, Tallahassee, Florida 32303. (1986). $7.95, pp. 170, 7-12. A women's hot romance in the summertime in New England. **

I'll Get There. It Better Be Worth the Trip., John Denovan, New York: Harper and Row, (1969). pp. 189, 6-12. Deals with an 11 years same sex encounter that ends positively.

Independence Day. B.A. Ecker, Avon Books. (1983). $2.25, pp. 208, 7-12. High school students discovering gay feelings.

In The Tent. David Rees, Boston: Alyson Pub. (1983). $6.85, pp. 130, 7-12. Growing up Catholic and Gay, mild deals with only feelings. **

Jack. A. M. Hone, New York: MacMillin Pub. Co., (1989). $13.95, pp. 220, 9-12, A family deals with divorce and a father's homosexuality in a loving story. ***

Kindred Spirits. Jeffrey M. Elliot (Ed.), Alyson Publications. $7.00, 7-12. Science Fiction dealing with gays and lesbian in other times and other worlds.

Legende: The Story of Philppa and Aurelie. Jeannine Allard, Boston: Alyson Publications. (1984). $5.95, pp. 125, 7-12. Historical fiction or nonfiction??? no one is sure.

Lucking In Love. Don Saherr, Boston: Alyson Pub. (1987). $5.95

Male Muse, The :Gay Poetry Anthology. Robert Duncan, et al, Crossing Press. (1973). $7.95, pp. 128, 7-12. Contemporary Anthologies Series

Milkman's On His Way, The. David Rees, London Gay Men's Press and Alyson Press. (1982). $7.95, pp. 118, 7-12. A young gay boy grows up with accepting friends. **

Maurice. E.M. Foster, Norton. (1987). $4.95, pp. 256, 9-12. Young gay male in pre-WWI England finds true lasting love. Movie is excellent - contains male nudity. ***

My Deep Dark Pain is Love: A Collection of Latin American Gay Fiction. E.A. Lacey, translated from Spanish and Port., Gay Sunshine Press. (1983). $10.00, pp. 384

Night Kites. M.E. Kerr, Harper Publ. $2.75, 6-10. A high school boy deal with his older bothers who has AIDS. **

Now That I Know. Norma Klein, Bantam. (1988). $2.95. A high school girl recognizes her father is gay, parents divorced.

Patience and Sarah. Fawcett Miller, (1983). $2.95, pp. 217, 8-12. If it was about a man and a woman and not two women, it would be required high school reading.
•••

Pearls, The. Shelley Smith, Naiad Press, P.O. Box 10543, Tallahassee, FL 32302. (1987). $7.95. pp. 165, 9-12.

Pink Triangle & Growing Up Gay: Retrospective Gay Fiction. J. Michael Clark, (Ed.). Lib Arts Press. (1987). $5.95.

Places, Please! The First Anthology of Lesbian Plays. Kate McDermott, Spinsters Aunt Lute. (1986). $8.95, pp. 220, 9-12.

Ruby. Rosa Guy, New York: Viking. (1976). 6-12. Two Black girls romance is hinted at but not clearly defined. Self-esteem is stressed.

Sticks and Stones. Lynn Hall, Chicago: Follett. (1977). (NIP) pp. 220, 7-12. Takes place in rural Iowa, pictures of homophobia and ignorance.

Truth About Alex, The. Anne Snyder, Signet Books. (1981). $2.75, pp. 166, 7-12. As seen on the HBO special of the same title. High School Student's friendship is explored. Peer/parent pressure, and coming out are the main themes. •••

Trying Hard To Hear You. Sandra Scoppettone, Boston: Alyson Pub.(1974). $7.95, pp. 264, 7-12. Show how homophobia destroys lives.

What Happened to Mr. Forster?. Gary Bargar. New York: Houghton Mifflin/Clarion Books. (1981). pp. 171. A sixth grader living in Kansas City in the 1950's learns to question the actions of those around him when one of his favorite teachers is accused of being a homosexual.

Nonfiction

A Way of Love, A Way of Life: A Young Person's Introduction to What It Means to Be Gay. Frances Hanckel, Lothrop, Lee, & Shepeard. (1979). $11.50, pp. 188, 7-12. A comprehensive book on being gay written specifically for young people. ••

Another Kind of Love. Richard Woods, Knoll Publishing Co., Fort Wayne, Indiana. (1988).

Being Lesbian. Lorraine Trenchard, Boston: Alyson Pub. (1986). pp. 144. Good for Lesbian High School Students

Brother to Brother: New Writing by Black Gay Men. Essex Hemphill, Boston: Alyson. (1991). $8.95, 11-12. For the mature reader. Stories by black, gay men.

Changing Bodies, Changing Lives: A Book for Teens on Sex and Relationships. Ruth Bell, Random House. (1987). $19.95, 7-12. Sections dealing with homosexuality. ••

Coming Along Fine: Today's Gay Man and His World. Wes Muchmore, William Hansen, Boston: Alyson Publishing. (1986). $6.95, pp. 148. For those already out but also for those who need reassurance in High School.

Coming Out Right. Wes Muchmore, William Hansen, Boston: Alyson Publishing. (1982). $5.95, pp. 204, 7-12. A collections of coming out stories with suggestions.

Coming Out Stories, The. Wolfe Stanley, Watertown, Mass: Persephone Press. (1980). (NIP). Coming out stories by 41 lesbians.

Coming Out to Parents - A Two-Way Survival Guide for Lesbians and Gay Men and Their Parents. Mary Borhek, New York: Pilgrim Press. (1983). $9.95, pp. 224. How to overcome reactions by understanding and love. •••

Coping with AIDS/Facts and Fears. Morton L. Kurland, New York: The Rosen Publishing Group. (1987). $6.95, pp. 210, 7-12. Richly fact filled. See the following.

Coping with Your Sexual Orientation. Deborah Miller, Alex Waigandt, New York: The Rosen Publishing Group. (1990). $13.95. 102 pp. 7-12. Also in the series "COPING WITH ..." with 26 other topics. Excellent for junior high school students. It contains activities and excellent questions and answers sections. ••

Different Drummer: Homosexuality in America. Messner. (1986). $11.29, pp. 112, 7-12.

Familiar Faces, Hidden Lives. Brown Howard; New York: Harcourt, Brace, Jovanovich. (1989). $8.95, pp. 246, 9-12.

Fighting Back: The Struggle for Gay Rights. Sabra Holbrook, New York: Lodestar Books, E. P. Dutton. (1987). $13.95, pp. 128, 7-12. Written for the young reader.

Gay: What Teenagers Should Know About Homosexuality and the AIDS Crisis. Morton Hunt, Michael Di Capua Books; New York: Farrar, Straus, Giroux. (1987). $6.95, pp. 244, 9-12. Best book published in recent years. Good frank introduction. •••

Gay Liberation in the Eighties. Gough & Mac Nier, Longwood Pub. Group. (1985). $9.50, pp. 131, 7-12.

Growing Up Gay. Youth Liberation, Carrier Pigeon, 75 Kneeland St, Boston, MA, 02111. (1978). (NIP) 7-12. Gay teenagers stories, excellent. ••

Homosexuality As Viewed From Five Perspectives Marcia Wetsman, National Federation of PFLAG, 5715 16th St. NW, Washington, D.C. 20011. Overview of the way gay children, parents, families, counselors, and communities react to homosexuality.

Homosexuality: The Body or the Mind?. Mayetta L. Ford, New York: Vantage Press. (1992). $10.00, pp. 51, 7-12. Looks at Society's Perceptions, The Human Body, The Bible, The Endocrine System, the development process. Probably too detailed for many students.

How to be a Happy Homosexual:A Guide for Gay Men. Terry Sanderson, GMP Publishers, P.O. Box 247, London, UK N17 9QR. (1987). $7.95, pp. 143. Good for High School Students.

In the Life: A Black Gay Anthology. Joseph Beam, Boston: Alyson Publishing. (1986). $7.95, pp. 260, 9-12.

Lesbian Crossroads. Ruth Baetz, New York: Naiad Press. (1988).

Living The Spirit: A Gay American Indian Anthology. Will Roscoe (Ed.), St. Martin Press. (1988). $16.95, pp. 240, 10-12.

One Teenager in 10. Ann Heron (Ed.), Boston: Alyson Pub. and Wilson Pub. (1986). $3.95, pp. 120., 7-12. Writings by gay and lesbian youth, "I'm not alone!!" •••

On Being Gay. Brian McNaught, New York: St. Martin Press. (1988). $13.95, pp. 176. His personal thoughts on family, faith, and love (has educational video)

Our Right to Love: A Lesbian Resource Book. Ginny Vida, Prentice-Hall. (1978). (NIP) $10.95, pp. 318, 9-12.

Original Coming Out Stories, The. Ed Julia Penelope and Susan J. Wolfe, The Crossing Press, Freedom, California, 95019. (1989). pp. 308, 9-12. Autobiographical stories written by women coming out and being out, excellent. •••

Positively Gay. Betty and Leighton Berzon, Celestial Arts. (1984) $7.95, pp., 239, 7-12, Mediamix. Happy gays exist!!!

Revaluations: A Collection of Gay Male Coming Out Stories. Curtis Wayne, Boston: Alyson Pub. (1988). $7.95, pp. 200.

Safe Sex: Guidelines That Could Save Your Life. Michael Helquist, Rofes. (1986). 9-12. A simple presentation of the Facts.

Something to Tell You. Lorraine Trachard, London Gay Teenage Group, Trojan Press, 10a Bradbury St, Hackney, London N16 8Jn. (1984). 7-12.

Testimonies: A Collection of Lesbian Coming Out Stories. Sarah Holmes (Ed.), Boston: Alyson Publishing. (1988). $7.95, pp. 200, 10-12.

Understanding Sexual Identity: A Book for Gay Teens and Their Friends. Janice E. Rench, Minneapolis: Lerner Publication Co. (1990). pp. 56, 6-12. Special designed for the public school with reinforced binding. Belongs in every Junior High School! ••

174

When Someone You Know Is Gay. Susan and Daniel Cohen, M. Evans & Company. (1989). $13.95, 7-12. Especially for teens with gay friends. ***

Young, Gay, And Proud!. Sasha Alyson, Boston: Alyson Pub. (1985). $3.95, 7-12. Super, several copies belong in every high school. ***

Religion

And God Loves Each One. Ann Thompson Cook, Dumbarton United Methodist Church Task Force on Reconciliation, 3133 Dumbarton St., N.W., Washington, DC 20007. (1987). $4.95. Excellent dealing specifically with gay/lesbian youth. ** ***

Is The Homosexual My Neighbor:Another Christian View. Letha Sconzoni, Harper & Row. (1980). $8.95, pp. 208. Good at relating views.

Lord is my Shepherd & He Knows I'm Gay. Troy & Lucas Perry, Bantam. (NIP) 7-12

The New Testament and Homosexuality, Robin Scroggs, Fortress. (1983).

History

A Sense of Pride: The Story of Gay Games II. Roy M. Coe, Pride Publishing. (1986). $14.95, pp. 128.

Gay Men and Women Who Enriched The World. Thomas Cowan, New York: William Mulvey Inc.. (1989). $8.95, pp. 257. Positive role models throughout history. ** ***

Gay American History: Lesbians and Gay Men in the U.S.A.: A Documentary. Jonathan Katz, Avon or Meridian Book. (1992). $8.95, pp. 702.

Gay Decades, The. Leigh W. Rutledge. New York: A Plum Book. (1992). $12.00, pp. 384. Analysis of the gay history, year by year.

Hidden From History: Reclaiming the Gay and Lesbian Past. Martin Duberman, Martha Vicinus, and George Chauncey, Jr. (Eds.). (1989). $24.95, pp. 608. ***

Homosexuality: A History. Vern Bullough, New American Library. (1979). $4.95, pp. 196. Western Gay History deals mainly with men.

Looking at Gay and Lesbian Life. Warren Blumenfeld and Dave Raymond, Boston: Beacon Press. (1988). An encyclopedic wealth of information.

Mayor of Castro Street, The: The Life & Times of Harvey Milk. Randy Shilts, St. Martin Press. (1983). $1.95, pp. 388.

Men In The Pink Triangle, The. Heinz Heger, Boston: Alyson Pub. (1983). $5.95, pp. 120. Gay history including WW II information and Nazi Germany. ** ***

Other Victims: first-person stories of non-Jews persecuted by the Nazis, The. Ina R. Friedman. Houghton Mifflin Co. (1990). pp. 214. especially for adolescents. personal narratives of Christians, Gypsies, deaf people, homosexuals, and Blacks. **

Pink Triangle, The. Richard Plant, New York: Holt, Henry & Co. (1988). $9.95, pp. 272. True stories of homosexual prisoners in the Nazi concentration camps.

Surpassing the Love of Men: Love Between Women from the Renaissance to the Present. Lillian Faderman, Morrow. (1981). $12.95, pp. 488.

Woman + Woman: Attitudes Toward Lesbianism. Delores Klaich, New York: William Morris and Co. (1974). Deals with lesbians and their history and the lack of inclusion in history books.

BOOKS FOR EDUCATORS

Counseling

Counseling Lesbian and Gay Male Youth: Their Special Lives/Special Needs. Sage Bergstrom, Lawrence Cruz (Eds.), National Network of Runaway and Youth Services, 905 6th St. SW., Suite 411, Washington, DC 20024. (1983).

Counseling & Education for Practice with Gay and Lesbians Natalie J. Woodman, Irvington, 212-777-4100. (1988). $24.95.

Easing the Ache: Gay Men Recovering from Compulsive Behavior. David Crawford, E.P. Dutton. (1990). $18.95

Gay and Lesbian Youth, Gilbert Herdt, PhD (Ed.), New York: Harrington Park Press. (1989). $19.95, pp. 355. A collection of professional writing dealing with gay and lesbian youth in the United States and other countries.

Gay and Lesbian Youth: Expressions of Identity. Ritch C. Savin-Williams, New York: Hemisphere Pub. Corp. (1990). pp. 202. *

Gay Children Grow Up: Gender Culture & Gender Deviance. Joseph Harvey, Praeger. (1982). $35.00, pp. 288.

Growing Up Gay In A Dysfunctional Family. Rik Isensee. Prentice Hall. (1991). $12.99. pp. 240. Describes the traumatic and chaotic family history of millions of gay men, recovery and development of self-esteem is stressed throughout.

Homosexuality and Family Relations. Frederick Bozett and Marvin Sussman, Haworth Press. (1990). Marriage and Family Review Ser.: Vol. 14, No. 3/4. pp. 349.

Homosexuality-Heterosexuality: Concepts of Sexual Orientation. McWhirter etal., Oxford University Press, 200 Madison Ave, NY, NY 10016, 212-679-7300, Inc. (1990). Kinsey Institute Ser. $45.00. pp. 448.

I Thought People Like That Killed Themselves:Lesbians, Gay Men and Suicide. Eric E. Rofes, Grey Fox. (1973). $2.00, pp. 176.

Often Invisible: Counseling Gay & Lesbian Youth. Margaret S. Schneider, Central Toronto Youth Services, 1988, 27 Carilton St., 3rd floor, Toronto, Ontario, M5B1l2. (1988). $14.00, pp. 135. Part 1 deals with Understanding Homosexuality while Part 2 deals with Counseling Strategies and Issues. *

"Sissy Boy Syndrome" & the Development of Homosexuality, The. Richard Green, Yale University Press. (1987). $40.00, pp. 432.

Understanding the Male Hustler. Samuel M. Steward, New York: Haworth Press. (1991). $8.95. A serious study of male hustlers using experiential dialogue.

Curricula

A Guide to Leading Introductory Workshops on Homophobia. written and edited by members of The Campaign to End Homophobia, P.O. Box 819, Cambridge, MA 02139. (1990). $12.00, pp.46. Written for a facilitator with little experience, excellent activities.

As Boys Become Men: Learning New Male Role. Doug Cooper Thompson, New York: Irvington Pub. (1985). $12.00, pp. 85, Order from Campaign to End Homophobia. Learning activities to explore male role stereotypes for high schools and other programs working with youth.

Homophobia:Discrimination Based on Sexual Orientation. Gay and Lesbian Alliance Against Defamation/LA, P.O. Box 741346 (or 74136) Los Angeles, California 90004. (1989). pp. 27. Excellent curriculum used in Los Angeles Unified School District, modeled after The World of Difference Program. *

Homophobia and Education: How to Deal with Name-Calling. Leonate Gordon, from Interracial Books for Children Bulletin, Vol. 14, No 3 & 4, Resource Center for Educators, 1841 Broad Way, Suite 500, New York , NY 10023. (1983). $3.95, pp. 39. *

176

Multicultural Education Curriculum: Learning Activities for 7th & 8th Grade Social Studies Classes, NYC Board of Education, Office for the Lesbian and Gay Community, 52 Chambers St, Rm. 311, NY, NY, 10007, (212)566-7385, (Oct. 1989). pp. 61, 7-8. Nine units for 7th & 8th Grade SS, can be used in other classes. *

Mutual Caring, Mutual Sharing. Cooper Thompson, The Clinic, P.O. Box 791, Dover, NH 03820, tel: 603-749-2346. $12.00, pp. 55, 6-9. Integrating a wide scope of topics into sexuality education programs for adolescents, 16 units. Very little on homosexuality. Sex Ed is supported instead of a case of denial.

Opening Doors to Understanding and Acceptance. Compiled by Kathy Obear. The Campaign to End Homophobia, P.O. Box 819, Cambridge, MA 02139. $12.00, pp. 52. Lesson plans for workshops to combat homophobia, for the more experienced workshop leader. Contains a wide variety of activities. *

Prejudice and Pride. The Philadelphia Inquirer, Educational Supplement. (December 15, 1986). pp. 16, 5-9. Worksheets and information, looks at differences in race, sex, sexual orientation, age or disability can make people feel pride or prejudice. *

Surviving AIDS: Simple Answer to Complex Questions About AIDS and Adolescent Homosexuality. Yoakman. University of Minnesota, Youth AIDS Project. Adolescent Health Program, Box 721, University of Minnesota, Hospital and Clinic, Harvard Street at East River Road, Minneapolis, Minnesota 55455, 612-626-2220. (1991). $5.00, pp. 37.

Gay/Lesbian Educators

From Closet to Classroom...A Perspective on Gay and Lesbian Individual is U.S. Schools. Myrna R. Olson, University of North Dakota Bookstore, Box 8197 University Station, Grand Forks, ND 58202. (1986). 70 pp. Portrays the circumstance of gay teachers.

Lesbian in Front of the Classroom:Writing by Lesbian Teachers, The. Sarah-Hope Parmeter and Irene Reti (Eds.), her Books. (1986). $6.50. Five lesbian teachers describe their lives.

Open and Positive. Gay Teacher's Group London, 112 Broxholm Road, London SE27. (1978). $2.45, pp. 72. A teachers legal battle to be openly gay.

Socrates, Plato and Guys Like Me: Confessions of a Gay Schoolteacher. Eric Rofes, Boston: Alyson Pub. (1985). $6.95, pp. 163. Deciding to come out is addressed.

Special Teachers/Special Boys. Pete Fisher, New York: St. Martin's Press. (1979). $4.95, pp. 342, 9-teachers. Fiction about being an open gay teacher in H.S.

Resources

Affording Equal Opportunity to Gay and Lesbian Students Through Teaching and Counseling. National Education Association, Human and Civil Rights, 1201 Sixteenth Street, NW, Washington, D.C. 20036, (202) 822-7730. Free to NEA members. An excellent resource for those training educators for it contains detailed information for educators. *

Alternatives: A Gamed of Understanding. Alternatives, P.O. Box 1050, Amherst, MA01004-1050, 413-546-4523. A creative tool to educate and develop awareness on the issues of homosexuality and bisexuality.

Annotated Filmography of Selected Films with Lesbian and Gay Content. Council on Social Work Education, 1600 Duke St., Alexandria, VA, 22314, 703-683-8080. $4.50. Date not set.

Bridges of Respect:Creating Support for Lesbian and Gay Youth, Katherine Whitlock, Rachael Kamel (Eds.), written for the American Friends Service Committee, 1501 Cherry Street, Philadelphia, PA 19101. (1988). $7.95, pp. 97. Excellent Resource Book. *

Children's Rights Handbook. Youth Liberation Press. $3.50. Contains a section on growing up gay, good for school counselors.

Colorado Community Directory. (1992). Boulder: Pink Triangle Productions, P.O. Drawer 2270, Boulder, CO 80306. A partial listing of the g/l community. *

Coming Out of the Classroom Closet: Gay and Lesbian Students, Teachers and Curricula. Karen Harbeck (Ed.), New York: Harrington Park Press. (1992). pp. 273, A collections of several great paper and articles. A MUST in a limited collection. *

Gay Talk: A (Sometimes Outrageous) Dictionary of Gay Slang. Bruce Rodgens, Brown Books. (1972). $4.95

Growing Up Gay in the South: Race, Gender, & Journeys of the Spirit. James T. Sears. Haworth Press. (1990). $19.95, 329 pp. An excellent resource for information. Written by a noted researcher. SUPERIOR!

Growing Healthy: AIDS Integration Grade K-7. Rocky Mountain Training Institute, 7525 West 10th Avenue, Lakewood, CO 80215-5191, 303-239-6494. This Aids supplement to Growing Healthy provides information about HIV and AIDS in the context of total wellness, decision-making, and skills for resisting peer pressure.

Haworth Press Inc., 10 Alice Street, Binghamton, NY 13904-1580, 1-800-3-HAWORTH. Publishes professional research on gay/lesbian issues. Ask for a Trade Catalog.

HIV/AIDS UPDATE, Spring, 1992. Colorado Department of Education, HIV/AIDS Prevention Project, 201 East Colfax, Denver, CO 80203, *Middle School Students and HIV Prevention Education*. Gives resources for curricula and study guides.

HIV/AIDS UPDATE, Winter 1992. Colorado Department of Education, HIV/AIDS Prevention Project, 201 East Colfax, Denver, CO 80203. *AIDS Education in the Elementary School*. Detailed listing of resources for elementary school teachers.

Homophobia: How We All Pay the Price. Warren J. Blumenfeld (Ed.), Boston: Beacon Press. (1992). $17.00, pp. 310. Deals will aspects of homophobia. An excellent section dealing with youth "It Has Nothing to Do With Me."

Lesbian and Gay Lifestyles. A Guide for Counseling and Education. Natalie J. Woodman, Irvington. (1992). $29.95, pp. 255.

Lesbians and Gays in Education: Twenty-First Century Challenge. Sue McConnell-Celi, Edward, William, and Austin. (1991). $12.95, pp. 224.

Lesbian in Literature, The. Barbara Grier (3rd ed.), Naiad Press, Inc. (). $7.95, pp. 240. A comprehensive bibliography.

One Out of Ten Students. The Advisory Committee on Lesbian and Gay Adolescents of the Personal Liberty Fund of The New Jersey Lesbian and Gay Coalition.

Project 10 Handbook: Addressing Lesbian and Gay Issues in Our Schools. Friends of Project 10 , Inc., 7850 Melrose Ave., Los Angeles 90046. (1989). $7.00, pp. 75. A resource directory for teachers, guidance counselors, parents and school-based adolescent care providers. *

Recommended Books for Children Living in Lesbian and Gay Families. Gay and Lesbian Parents Coalition International, P.O. Box 50360, Washington, DC 20091, 202-583-8029. (1991). pp. 10. This bibliography contains books which are explicitly or implicitly lesbian or gay, single mothers, single fathers, lesbian/gay parents, AIDS, sex roles, sexual identity, and positive self images. Excellent.

Serving Gay and Lesbian Youths: the Role of Child Welfare Agencies, Recommendations from a CWLA Colloquim. Child Welfare League of America Staff. Child Welfare. (1991). $6.95.

178

Sexual Minority Youth: An At Risk Population. The Taskforce on Sexual Minority
    Youth, Portland, Oregon. Ten copies provided by the NEA to each state affili-
    ate. *
Sexual Orientation and the Law. Harvard Law Review. Harvard University Press, 79
    Garden St., Cambridge, MA 02138, 617-495-2600. (1990). $9.95, 192pp.
Talking About School. Hugh Warren, London Gay Teenage Group. (1984). $6.75, pp.
    48, Available from Giovanni's Room, 1145 Pine Street, Philadelphia, PA
    19107. Examines school curriculum and attitudes of educators in London,
    England.
What Kids Need to Know About AIDS: Resources and Life Skills Exercises for
    Educator K-6. Planned Parenthood of North East Pennsylvania, 112 North
    13th St., Allentown, PA 19101. (1988). $7.95, p. 97. Excellent basic resource
    book.

179

BOOKS FOR PARENTS

A Family Matter: A Parent's Guide to Homosexuality. Charles Silverstein, McGraw-Hill. (1981). $7.95, pp. 214, 7-12. Very gentle

Are You Still My Mother? Are You Still My Family?. Gloria Guss Back, Warner Books. (1985). $7.95, pp. 233, 7-12. A must for parents or students. *

Beyond Acceptance. Writh et al, Prentice-Hall. (1986). $16.95, pp. 272, 9-12. Parents of gay children write, loving is beyond acceptance. *

Bibliography on Gays and Lesbians and Their Families, A. Michael Waterman, The Gay and Lesbian Parents Coalition International, P.O. Box 50360, Washington DC 20019, 202-583-8029. (1991). pp. 20. Excellent bibliography. Contains information on Gay Fathers, Lesbian Mothers, Step-Parents, Heterosexual Spouses, Children of Homosexual Parents, General Interest.

Consenting Adult. Laura Hobson, Warner. (1976). $3.50, pp. 288, 9-12. Support for parents of gay children, gay history.

Different Daughters: A Book by Mothers of Lesbians. Louise Rafkin, Cleis Press. (1987). $8.95, pp. 160.

Final Closet: The Gay Parents Guide for Coming Out to Their Children. Rip Corley, Miami: Editech Press. (1990).

Gay & Lesbian Parents. Frederick Bozett (Ed.), Praeger. (1987). $14.95, pp. 263.

Gay Youth: A Positive Approach for Parents & Sibling. Brownley, Comm Intervention. (1988). $3.95, pp. 30.

Goodbye, I Love You. Carol Lynn Pearson, Jove Books. (1986).

Growing Up Free: Raising Your Kids in the 80's. Letty Cottin-Pogrebin, McGraw. (1980). $8.95. Contains a chapter: Not Being A Homophobic Parent.

Homosexuality and the Family. Fredrick Bozett, Binghamton, NY: Harrington Park Press. (1989). $17.95. Deals with a variety of issues from youth to family.

Living with and Loving Your Gay Child. Karen Baker and James Windell, Minerva Press, 6653 Andersonville Road, Waterford, MI 48095. (1988). pp. 14. A good but brief resource written by a social worker and a psychotherapist.

My Son Eric. Mary Bothek, New York: Pilgrim Press. (1984). pp. 160, 7-12. For parents of gay children, Christian belief system.

New Loving Someone Gay, The. Don Clark, Signet Books (National American Library), NY, Celestial Arts. (1987). $7.50, pp. 292, 9-12. Supports parents with gay children by discussing facts.

Now That You Know: What Every Parent Should Know About Homosexuality. Betty Fairchild, San Diego: Harcourt Brace Jovanovich. (1988). $6.95, pp. 240. A classic written by the founder of Parent & Friends of Lesbian and Gays.

Other Side of the Closet, The. Amity Pierce Buxton, IBS Press. (1991). $14.95. Offers guidelines to help the straight spouse whose loved one has come out.

Parents Matter: Parents' Relationships with Lesbian Daughters & Gay Sons. Ann Muller, Naiad Press. (1987). $9.95, pp. 218.

Parents Of The Homosexual. David and Shirley Surtzer, Christian Care Books, Philadelphia: The Westminster Press & John Know. (1980). $7.95, pp. 118. A must for extremely religious Christian parents. A first step. *

There's Something I've Been Meaning to Tell You: An Anthology About Lesbians & Gay Men coming Out to Their Children. Laralee MacPike, editor. Naiad Press. (1989). $9.95

We Are Everywhere. Alpert Harriet, Freedom, CA: The Crossing Press. (1988). $10.95. A collection of writing by lesbian parents.

Whose Child Cries. Joe Gantz, Jalma Press. (1983). $8.95, pp. 272. Children of gay parents speak out. *

ARTICLES
Popular Print

America's Worst Kept Secret - Teen Sex. The Advocate. Victoria A. Brownworth. (1992, March). Issue 599. pp. 38-46.

Attitudes Toward Homosexuality. Parents, Dr. David Elkind. (1991, August).

Barrierss Fail To Keep Student From Success: Gay, poor but determined, she found racial bias toughest hurdle. The Denver Post, Mark Stevens. (1992, July 12). •

Books Help Children of Gay Parents. New York Times. Heather Harlan. (1992, April 5). Vol. 141, p. ED8.

Coming Out Now. Newsweek. James N. Baker. (1990, Summer/Fall - special edition) Vol. 115, No. 27, pp. 60-62.

Experts Say Problems of Gay Teens Begin With Fear of Telling Parents. The Denver Post. Mary Kasdan. (1986, Nov 5).

For Gay Students, No Place to Turn. The Denver Post. Mark Stevens. (1990, Dec 2). •

Future of Gay America, The. Newsweek. (1990, March 12). pp. 20-27.

Gay Americas in Transition. Newsweek. (1983, Aug 8). pp. 30-40.

Gay Youth Slipping Through the Cracks. Guide Magazine. Gary Sanford. (1987, May). pp. 17-18.

Gays Achieving Mainstream 'Normalcy' in TV Portrayals. The Denver Post. Joanne Ostrow. (1991, June 9).

Gays and Lesbians are Entitled to Respect. The Denver Post. Penelope Purdy. (1992, Oct 21).

Gays and Lesbians in Therapy: You Can Go Home Again. Networker. Laura M. Markowits. (1991, Jan/Feb). pp. 55-60.

Gays in School. The Washington Post. Patrick Welsh. (1990, March 4).

Hate Crimes Against Gays Rise. The Denver Post. Larry Johnson. (1992, March 20).

Hate In America. Scholastic Update. (1992, April 3). Vol. 124, No. 14. •

Homophobia in Schools on What We Don't Know will Hurt Us. unknown. Pam Chamberlain.

Homosexual Parents Debut in Kid's Book. The Denver Post. Sheila Anne Feeney. (1991, Jan).

Hundreds Turn Out for Soviet Gay Events. OutFront. Rex Vockner. (1991, Aug 16). pp. 10

Hypothalamus Study and Coverage of It Attracts Many Barbs. Advocate. John Galla-
gher. (1991, Oct 8). pp. 14-15

Is This Child Gay? Born or Bred: the Origins of Homosexuality. Newsweek. (1992, Feb
24). pp. 46-53. *

New Teens, The. Newsweek. (1990 Summer/Fall). pp. 60-61.

Place to be Somebody: at Harvey Milk School, gays and lesbians are the norm, A. Time.
Kathleen Brady. (1989, Nov. 13). Vol. 134, No. 20, pp. 21-24.

Perpetual Sunset: Soviet Gays. Frontier. Bill Strubbe. (1991, Sept 3). pp. 31-36.

Romer Bans Bias Based On Sexual Orientation. The Denver Post. (1990, Dec 15).

Some Die Young. The Washington Blade. Fred Parris. (1985, May). Vol. 16, No. 20.

Straight or gay? Researchers are unraveling the origins of homosexuality. Parent's
Magazine. David and Barbara Bjorklund. (1988, Oct). Vol.63, No. 10, pp. 93-
98.

Study Finds Brains of Gay, Straight Men Differ. The Denver Post. Natalie Angier.
(1991, Aug 30).

Suicide cited as leading cause for death among young gay men and lesbians. Gay
Community News. John Zeh. (1989, Oct 22-28). p. 3.

Teen Age Homosexuality. The Washington Post. Marguritte Kelly. (1985, Nov 1).

Teen Suicide. The Advocate. Shira Magues. (1991, Sept 24, 586). pp. 40-47.

Variations On a Theme. Newsweek Special Issue. Seligmann. (1990, Winter/Spring).
p. 47.

What Causes People to Be Homosexual. Newsweek. Sharon Begley. (1991, Sept 9).

Young Gays and AIDS - The Second Wave. Out Front. Jonathan Mitchell. (1992,
March 4). pp. 12-13.

Youth Guilty of Hate Crime in Beating of Gay Neighbor. New York Times. (1991, Aug
17). Vol. 140, p. 8.

Professional Print

A Homosexual Teacher's Argument and Plea, Phi Delta Kappan. (1977, Oct). pp. 53-
54.

A Very Silent and Gay Minority. School Counselor. Gloria J. Krysiak. (1987, March).
Vol. 34, No. 4, Pp. 304-307.

*Addressing the Needs of Lesbian, Gay, and Bisexual Youth: the Origins of PROJECT 10
and school-based intervention.* Journal of Homosexuality. V. Uribe and K.M.
Harbeck. (1992). Vol. 22, No. 3-4, pp. 9-28.

Adolescent Homosexuality. Clinical Pediatrics. Gary J. Remafedi. (1985, Sept). pp.
481-485.

Adolescent Homosexuality: Psycholsocial and Medical Implications. <u>Pediatrics</u>. G.J. Remafedi. (1987, March). Vol. 79, No. 3, pp. 331-337.

AIDS in Adolescence. <u>Journal of Adolescent Health Care</u>. Karen Hein, MD. (1989, 10, 105-355).

Assessing and Addressing the Special Challenge of Gay and Lesbian Students for High School Counseling Programs. Presented at the Annual Meeting of the California Educational Research Association. Anne C. Benvenuti. (1986, Nov 14). pp. 14. ERIC Document Reproduction Service, ED279958. *

Attitudes, Experiences, and Feelings of Guidance Counselors in Working with Homosexual Students: A Report on the Quality of School Life for Southern Gay and Lesbian Students. Presented at the Annual Meeting of the American Educational Research Association. James T. Sears. (1988, April). ERIC document Reproduction Service, ED292610.

Biphobia. <u>Empathy</u>. Marcia Deihl and Robyn Ochs. (1989/90, Fall/Winter). Vol. 2, No. 1, pp. 15-19.

Caring for Gay and Lesbian Youth: Homosexual teenagers have special needs and concerns that are best addressed by a supportive physician whom they can trust.... <u>Medical Aspects of Human Sexuality</u>. Kevin Cwayna. (1991, July 1). Vol. 25, No. 7, p. 50.

Chinese Homosexuals Marry Despite Ban. <u>Japan Economic News</u>. (1989, Feb. 2).

Coming Out in the Gay World. <u>Psychiatry</u>. Dank, B. (1971, May). Vol. 34, pp. 180-197.

Coming Out Process for Homosexuals, The. <u>Hosp. Community Psychiatry</u>. H.P. Martin. (1991, Feb). Vol. 42, No. 2, pp. 158-162.

Coming Out to Parents and Self-Esteem Among Gay and Lesbian Youths, <u>Journal of Homosexuality</u>. Ritch C. Savin-Williams. Vol. 18, No. 1-2, pp. 1-35. *

<u>Construction of Homosexuality, The</u>. David Greenberg. University of Chicago Press. (1990). pp. 638, $17.95.

<u>Counseling Psychologist, The</u>. (1991). Vol. 19, No. 2, pp. 156-252. Several articles: basic scientific and therapeutic work, lesbian women, gay men, issues in counseling psychology training.

Counseling Special Populations: The Invisible Minority. Sara Rydberg, graduate paper for Ed.D., (1987). unknown.

Don't Pass Us By: Keeping Lesbian and Gay Issues on the Agenda. <u>Gender and Education</u>. Jane Andrews. (1990). Vol. 2, No. 3, pp.51-55.

Educated To Be Invisible: The Gay and Lesbian Adolescent. Katheryn L. Dunham. (1989). pp. 26. ERIC ED336676.

Educators, Homosexuality, and Homosexual Students: Are Personal Feelings Related to Professional Beliefs?. <u>Journal of Homosexuality</u>. James Sears. (1992) Vol. 22, No. 3-4, pp. 29-79.

Educational Responsibilities to the Gay and Lesbian Student. Presented at the Annual Meeting of the Speech Communication Association. Joseph A. DeVito. (1970, November) 25 pp. ERIC Document Reproduction Service (EDRS) ED 184 167, CS 502 842, (1979).

Faggot in the Woodpile: Teaching Gay Students, The. Paper Presented at the Annual Meeting of the College English Assn. Louie Crew. (1975, April 12). 13 pp. ERIC, ED 119 236, CS 202 568.

From Hiding Out to Coming Out: Empowering Lesbian and Gay Educators. Journal of Homosexuality. Pat Griffin. (1992). Vol. 22, No. 3/4, pp. 167-96.

Fundamental Issues in the Care of Homosexual Youth. Medical Clinic of North America. Gary Remafedi. (1990, Sept). Vol. 74, No. 5, p. 1169.

Gay and Lesbian Adolescents Marriage and Family Review. Journal of Homosexuality. (1989). Vol. 14, No. 3/4, pp. 197-216.

Gay and Lesbian Educators: Past History/Future Prospects. Journal of Homosexuality. K.M. Harbeck (1992). Vol. 22, No. 3-4, pp. 121-140.

Gay and Lesbian Teen: A Case of Denied Adolescence, The. Journal of Pediatric Health Care. Robert Bidwell, (1988, Jan/Feb). Vol. 2, No. 1, pp. 3-8.

Gay and Lesbian Youth. Planning to Live: Suicidal Youths in Community Setting. Joyce Hunter and Robert Schaecher. (1990). pp. 297-317. Tulsa: University of Oklahoma Press

Gay and Lesbian Youths and Their Parents. Empathy. Ritch Savin-Williams. (1989/90, Fall/Winter). Vol. 2, No. 1, pp. 41-42.

Gay Identity Issues Among Black Americans: Racism, Homophobia, and the Need for Validation. Journal of Counseling & Development. Darryl K. Loiacano. (1989, Sept/Oct). Vol. 68, pp. 21-25.

Gay Kids, Mad Parents; Many young Homosexuals Face Hostility on the Home Front, American Health: Fitness of Body and Mind. Judy Folkenberg. (1989, Dec). Vol. 8, No. 10, pp. 78-80.

Gay, Lesbian, and Bisexual Adolescents: A Critical Challenge to Counselors. Journal of Counseling & Development. Eli Coleman and Gary Remafedi. (1989, Sept/Oct). Vol. 68, No. 1, pp. 36-40. •

Gay-Lesbian Patient and the Family Physician, The. Journal of Family Practice. Ansteet, Kiernan, Brown. (1987). Vol. 25, No. 4, pp. 339-344.

Gay Youth and the Right to Education. Yale Law & Policy Review. Donna I. Dennis and Ruth E. Harlow. (1986, Spring/Summer). Vol. 4, No. 2, pp. 446-477. •

Gays and Lesbians in Therapy: You Can Go Home Again. Networker. Laura M. Markowity. (1991, Jan/Feb). pp. 55-60.

Health Care Delivery and the Concerns of Gay and Lesbian Adolescents. Journal of Adolescent Health Care. Paul A. Paroski. (1987). Vol. 8, No. 2, pp. 188-192.

184

Hispanic Culture, Gay Male Culture, and AIDS: Counseling Implications. Journal of Counseling & Development. Alex Carballo-DiEguez. (1989, Sept/Oct). Vol. 68, pp. 26-30.

Homosexual Adolescent: Developmental Issues and Social Bias, The. Child Welfare, Alan Malyon. (1981, May). pp. 321- 331.

Homosexual and Counseling, The. Personnel and Guidance Journal. Norton. (1976, March). Vol. 54, pp. 374-377.

Homosexual Behavior and the School Counselor. The School Counselor. Robert Earl Powell. (1987, Jan). Vol. 34, No. 3, pp. 202-208.

Homosexual Educator: Past History/Future Prospects, The. Presented at the Annual Meeting of the American Educational Research Association. Karen M. Harbeck. (1989, March) pp. 33. ERIC Document Reproduction Service, ED3220169.

Homosexual Teacher's Argument and Plea, A. Phi Delta Kappan. Anonymous. (1977, Oct). pp. 93-94.

Homosexual Youth: A Challenge to Contemporary Society. JAMA. Gary Remafedi. (1987, July 10). Vol. 258, No. 2, pp. 222-225. *

Homosexuality and Adolescence. Pediatrics. American Academy of Pediatrics Committee on Adolescence. (1983). Vol. 72, pp. 249-250.

Homosexuality and Public Education. West's Education Law Reporter. Walden, J. & Culverhouse, R. (1989). Vol. 55, No. 1, pp. 7-33.

Homosexuality, Counseling and the Adolescent Male. Personnel and Guidance Journal. E. Kremer, D. Zimpfer, and T. Wigger. (1975). Vol. 54, pp. 94-99.

Homosexuality in Adolescence. Seminars in Adolescent Medicine. D.E. Greydanus and D. Dewdny. (1985). Vol. 1, pp. 117-129.

In Defense of Gay Lessons. Journal of Moral Education. J. Martin Stafford. (1988, Jan). Vol. 17, No. 1, pp. 11-20. *

Including Curriculum Content on Lesbian and Gay Issues. Journal of Social Work Education. Bernie S. Newman. (1989, Fall). Vol. 25, No. 3, pp. 202-211. *

Inclusion, Not Exclusion: Recreation Service Delivery to Lesbian, Gay and Bisexual Youth. Journal of Adolescent Health. Gabe Kruks. (1991, Nov. 1). Vol. 63, No. 4 p. 45.

Issues of Identity Development Among Asian-American Lesbians and Gay Men. Journal of Counseling & Development. Connie S. Chan. (1989, Sept/Oct). Vol. 68, pp. 16-20.

Learning to Hide: The Socialization of the Gay Adolescent. Adolescent Psychiatry. A. Damien Martin. (1982). Vol. 10, pp. 52-65. University of Chicago Press.

Lesbian and Gay Educators: Opening the Classroom Closet. Empathy. Pat Giffin. (1992). Vol. 3, No. 1, pp. 25-28.

185

Male Homosexuality: The Adolescent's Perspective. Pediatrics. G.J. Ramefedi. (1987, March). Vol. 79, No. 3, pp. 326-330.

Medical Problems of the Homosexual Adolescents. Journal of Adolescent Health Care. William F. Owen, Jr., M.D. (1985:6). pp. 278-285.

Mental Health Issues of Gay and Lesbian Adolescents. Journal of Adolescent Health Care. John Gonsiorek. (1988:9). pp. 114-122.

Morin, S. Many articles on education and homosexuality
Homosexual Counseling Journal. (1974). Vol. 1 pp. 160-165.
American Psychologist. (1977). Vol. 32, No. 8. pp. 629-637.
Journal of Social Issues, (1978). Vol. 34, No. 1 , pp. 29-44.
Demystifying Homosexuality, (1978). Vol. 34(2), pp. 137-148.

Moving Through Loss:The Spiritual Journey of Gay Men and Lesbian Women. Journal of Counseling Development. Kathleen Y. Ritter and Craig W. O'Neill. (1989, Sept/Oct). Vol. 68, pp. 9-15.

Needs of Gay Students for Acceptance and Support, Education Digest. Gloria J. Krysiak. (1987, Dec). Vol. 53, No. 4, pp. 44-48.

Open Hands: *Opening the Closet Door.* Mark Bowman, pp. 11-14.
                                   The Children's World. Gregory Dell, pp. 15-16.
                                   Loving the Different Ones. Roger Dieheson.

Opening Up the Classroom Closet: Responding to the Educational Needs of Gay and Lesbian Youth. Harvard Educational Review. Eric Rofes. (1989, Nov). Vol. 59, No. 4, pp. 444-453. *

Personal Feelings and Professional Attitudes of Prospective Teachers toward Homosexuality and Homosexual Students: Research Findings and Curriculum Recommendations. Presented at the Annual Meeting of the American Educational Research Association. James. T. Sears. (1989, March). ERIC Document Reproduction Service, ED312222.

Preliminary Study of Social Issues in AIDS Prevention Among Adolescents, A. Journal of School Health. Michael Ross, Chris Caudle, Julie Taylor. (1989, Sept). Vol. 59, No. 7, pp. 308-311.

Psychoanalytic Perspective of Adolescent Homosexuality. Adolescence. Jon. K. Mills. 1990, Winter) Vol. 25, No. 100, pp. 913-923.

Reach Them and Teach Them. Teachers Magazine. (1990, May). pp. 34-35.

Reactions of Gay and Lesbian Youth to Verbal and Physical Harassment. Human Ecology Forum. Ritch C. Savin-Williams. (1990, Winter). Vol. 18, No. 2, pp. 12-14.

Reducing Homophobia Among Educators and Students. Education Digest. Rober Schaecher. (1989, April). Vol. 54, No. 8, pp. 58-64. *

Report of the Secretary's Task Force on YOUTH SUICIDE. Volume 3, U.S. Department of Health and Human Services. (1989, Jan). pp. 3-110 to 3-142. **

Risk Factors for Attempted Suicide in Gay and Bisexual Youth. Pediatrics. G. Remafedi. (1991, June). Vol. 87, No. 6, p. 869.

School Districts Reach Out to Gay and Lesbian Youth. School Board News. National School Boards Associations. Erica Gordon Sorohan. (1990, June 19). Vol. 10, No. 11.

Staff Development Program for Anti-homophobia Education in the Secondary Schools. Authur Samuel Lipkin. University of Massachusetts, Ed.D. (1990) pp. 266. UMI ADG91-0523. DAI V51(08), SECA, PP2713. Assess the impact of a twelve-hour anti-homophobia workshop on the attitudes and professional practice of 16 staff participants at a public high school in Cambridge, MA.

Stigmatization of the Gay and Lesbian Adolescent, The. Journal of Homosexuality. Damien Martin and Emery Hetrick. (1988). Vol. 15, Numbers 1/2, New York University, Harworth Press, pp. 163-183. *

Straight Scoop: Homophobia and Male Isolation Patterns, The. Brotherbond: Newsletter of the National Organization for Changing Men. Washington, D.C. Gerry Sutter. (1988, June). No. 10.

Stresses on Lesbian and Gay Adolescents. Independent School. Robert Schaecher. (1989, Winter). Vol. 48, No. 2, pp. 29-31.

Stresses on Lesbian and Gay Adolescents. Social Work in Education. Joyce Hunter and Robert Schaecher. (1987, Spring). Vol. 9, No. 3, pp. 180-189. The National Association of Social Workers. *

Suicidal Behavior in Adolescent and Young Adult Gay Men. Suicide and Life-Treating Behavior. Schneider et al. (1989, Winter). Vol. 19, pp. 393-396.

Survey to Examine the Relationships Between the Openness of Self-identified Lesbian, Gay Male, and Bisexual Public School Teachers to Job Stress and Job Satisfaction. Thomas Patrick Juul. New York: New York University, School of Education, Health, Nursing, Art Profession. (1992, December). *

Talking About Lesbians/Gays in "Regular" High School History: Journal Reflections. Empathy. Kevin Jennings. (1992). Vol. 3, No. 1, pp. 29-31.

Teaching About Homosexuality. Independent School. Paul Williams. (1989, Winter). Vol. 48, No. 2, p. 17.

Teaching Assertive Skills to a Passive Homosexual Adolescent. Journal of Homosexuality. McKinley, et al. (1977). Vol. 3, No. 2, pp. 163-170.

Teaching Gay Students. Association for Supervision and Curriculum Development Update. Scott Willis. (1991, March).

Television Viewing an Adolescents' Sexual Behavior. Journal Of Homosexuality. Jane D. Brown and Susan F. Newcomer. (1991, Jan/Feb). Vol. 21, No. 1-2, pp. 77-82.

Violence Against Lesbian and Gay Male Youths. Journal of Interpersonal Violence. (1990, Sept). Vol. 5, No. 3, pp. 295-300.

What Every M.D. Needs to know About Gay Teen-agers (includes related article on counseling services). <u>Medical Economics</u>. Gary Remafedi. (1990, July 23). Vol. 67, No. 14, pp. 113-119.

What About Gay Teenagers?. <u>Journal of Dis Child</u>. Fikar. (1991, Mar). Vol. 145, No. 3, p. 252.

Working with Lesbian and Gay Youth. <u>Adolescent Sexuality Report</u>. Robert Scaecher. (1988, July/Aug).

188

FILM/VIDEO/AUDIO

A Merchant Ivory Film, 34 South Mohon Street, London, WTY 2BP, England

Maurice, video, color, 1987, A full length movie dramatizing E.M. Forester award
    winning novel. A young man come to terms with his gay identity set in Historic
    London. Excellent, contains 10 sec of male nudity. Available at most video
    stores.

Cambridge Documentary Films, P.O. Box 385, Cambridge MA 02139; (617) 354-2677

Choosing Children, rent 16mm, 45 min. Changing definitions of family by interview-
    ing lesbians mothers.
Pink Triangles, rent 35mm, Documents homophobia and discrimination against gay
    and lesbians through personal interviews.

Cinecom, 1250 Broadway, New York, NY 10001; (212) 629-6222

The Times of Harvey Milk, rent 16mm or video for public performances, 87 min,
    color, also available in video rental stores. Academy Award winning documen-
    tary about the life and death of San Francisco City Supervisor Harvey Milk.
    Available in some video stores. *

Cinema Guild, 1697 Broadway, Suite 802, New York, NY 10019; (212) 246-5522

Before Stonewall: The Making of a Gay and Lesbian Community, purchase 16mm -
    $1200 or video - $695, rental $125, 87 min., color/B&W, purchase VHS for
    $29.95. Social, political and cultural development of the gay and lesbian
    community is analyzed in detailed. History of homosexual experience in
    America. Two Emmy Awards (book also)
Not All Parents Are Straight, purchase 16mm - $895 or video - $595, rent $95, 58
    min., 1986, color, purchase VHS $39.95. Interviews with children and their gay
    and lesbian parents. Viewers will be forced to confront their own unexamined
    assumptions or biases.

Cinevista, 353 W. 39th Street, New York, NY 10018

Improper Conduct, rent 35mm, 115 min. Traces the oppression of gays during Cas-
    tro's Cuban Revolution by documenting the victims.

Coronet/MTI File & Video, 108 Vilmot Road, Deerfield, IL 60015; (708) 940-1260

The Truth About Alex, video purchased for $250, 1989, two versions - 30 or 50 min.,
    color. It's discovered that high school football star Alex is gay, his best friend
    Brad courageously supports him. HBO Special starring Scott Baio and Peter
    Spence, Brad faces a choice of standing by his gay friend or losing a West Point
    appointment with homophobia from parents, friends, teammates. (book: The
    Truth About Alex, original title: Counterplay) *
What If I'm Gay?: A Search for Understanding, video purchased for $250, 1988, two
    versions - 30 or 46 min., color, CBS Schoolbreak Special. Dramatized is a
    teenage boy who ponders how his realization and acceptance of his gayness will
    affect his friends and family, and how it may shape the course of his future.
    CINE Golden Eagle; Silver, National Education; Chris Bronze Plaque, Colum-
    bus International Film Festivals; National Council on Family Relations. *

Equity Institute, Tucker-Taft Building, 48 North Pleasant St., Amherst, MA 01002, (413) 256-0271.

Sticks, Stones and Stereotypes, Purchase - $450, Curriculum module/ Teachers Guide - purchase $200. Name calling is explored. With Spanish/English subtitles. *

Fanlight Production, 47 Halifax St., Boston, MA 02130, (617) 524-0980.

First Dance, Purchased - $240, rental $50/$100, color. Based on REFLECTIONS OF A ROCK LOBSTER, an effective introductory tool for teachers.

Federation of Parents and Friends of Lesbians and Gays, 1012 Fourteeth Street, NW, Suite 700, Washington, DC 20005:

First write for a listing of audio tapes available, topics include:
Parents and their children
Youth
Religious Issues *and many more.*

Filmmakers Library, 124 East 40th Street, #901, New York, NY, 10025; (212) 355-6545, 133 E. 58th St., NY, NY, 10022

Michael, a Gay Son, rent 16mm - $55, 27 min., 1981, color. Gives insight about coming out to unprepared family members, great for professionals.
Out in Suburbia: The Stories of Eleven Lesbians, rent video - $55, 28 min., 1989 color. shows us many lesbians who have mainstream values and lead conventional lives. Discussion guide available.
Silent Pioneers, rent 16mm or video - $65, two versions - 30 or 42 min., 1985, 6 lesbian and gay elders.
We Are Family, rent video -$75, 57 min., 1987, color, Three non-traditional families, you realize that good parenting is independent of sexual orientation.

Focus International

Early Homosexual Fears, 11min. b/w, Girls and boys discuss the concerns about experimenting with homosexual activities.

Friends of Project 10, Inc., 7850 Melrose Ave., Los Angeles 90046, (818) 441-3382 and (213) 651-5200

Who's Afraid of Project 10?, video purchased, 1989, 23 min., color. Documentary featuring compelling interviews with Dr. Uribe, students, parents, and elected officials.

Lambda Rising, 1625 Connecticut Ave., N.W., Washington, D.C. 20009-1013; (202) 462-6969.

Parting Glances, Video purchased, A man must say goodbye to his lover leaving for Africa and to a close friend dying with AIDS.
Therese and Isabelle, Video purchased, First love of young girls in the shadows of an all girls school. Available in some video stores.
The Times of Harvey Milk, Video purchased, Academy Award winning documentary about the life and death of San Francisco City Supervisor Harvey Milk.
You Are Not Alone, Video purchased, foreign film with subtitles, excellent

McGraw-Hills Films, 110 15th Street, Del Mar, CA 92014; (619) 481-8184

What About McBride?, rent or purchase 16mm, 10 min., color, Two boys discuss
whether to invite McBride on a rafting trip. McBride is rumored to be gay and
one teenage boy objects. The point is argued but left unresolved. Several questions are poised at the end to the audience.

Moonforce Media, attn. Joan Byron, P.O. Box 2934, Washington, D.C. 20012; (202)
526-0049

For Love and For Life: The 1987 March on Washington for Lesbian and Gay Rights,
Video purchased or slideshow format. Brief history of the liberation movement
and a photographic of the March on Washington and related events.

New Yorker Films, 16 West 61st Street, New York, NY 10023; (212) 247-6110

The Word is Out: Stories of Some of Our Lives, rent 16mm, 2 versions - 45 or 130
min., An absorbing documentary of 26 gays and lesbians.

Other Cinema, Little Newport Street, London WC1

Veronica for Rose, positive images of young lesbians are explored by interviews.
True Romance, positive images of same-sex relationships along with heterosexual.

Parents and Friends of Lesbian and Gays - Denver, P.O. Box 18901, Denver, CO
80218

An Unexpected Journey, video, purchased $25, approx. 30 min., 1991, color. Shows
the lives of several gay/lesbian youth. An Excellent resource for trainers.

TRB Productions, New Ways Ministry, 4012 29th St. Mr. Rainier, MD 20712

A Conversation With Brian McNaught: On Being Gay, video purchase, 2 parts - 80
min., 1986, color, Brian McNaught, a award winning author and lecturer,
explores growing up gay and his own youth. (related book On Being Gay by
Brian McNaught)

Women Make Movies, Inc., 225 Lafayette Street, #212, New York, NY 10012; (212)
925-0606

A Woman of My Platoon, purchase 16 mm - $250 video - $200, rental - $50, 20 min.
1989, color, Looks at women's experience in Canada's military during WW II.
Three parts: 1) lesbian's dishonorable discharge 2) Counters with classic
wartime footage of women 3) Bill voted down to prevent discrimination
Greeting From Washington, purchase 16mm - $500 or video - $275, rental - $60,
1979, 28 min., color. Outlines the first National Gay and Lesbian Rights March
in Washington, D.C.
Honored by the Moon, purchase video - $150, rent - $50, 1990, 15 min., color, Mona
Smith, Native American Lesbians and Gays speak of their unique historical
and spiritual role. Upbeat and empowering videotape.
In The Best Interest of the Children, purchase 16mm - $750 or video - $250, rent
16mm - $100 video - $75, 53 mins., color, Eight diverse lesbian mothers discuss
the issues of child custody and lesbian parents.
Just Because of Who We Are, purchase video - $195, rent video - $60, 28 min., 1986,
color. Explores the physical and psychological harassment directed at lesbians.

Lifetime Commitment: A Portrait of Karen Thompson, purchase video - $195, rental - $60, 30 min., color. In 1983 her lover was critically injured, since then she has been fighting to see Sharon and care for her. Acting for legal and social change.

Storme: The Lady of the Jewel Box, rent 16mm or video, 21 min. Storme DeLaverie is profiled as a male impersonator and extraordinary woman. Black and gay history is investigated.

Susana, purchase 16mm - $500 or video - $225, rental - $75, 25 min., 1980, color, A young Argentine lesbian growing up in a homophobic environment.

You Can Fight City Hall, purchase video - $195, rental - $60, 1986, 30 min., color. A fight to add sexual orientation, Columbus Ohio City Council meeting. A grim awakening to the homophobia and catalyst for action and change.

Television

KBDI - TV, Box 427, Broomfield, CO 80020

Half Million Strong, purchase video - $30, approx 1 hr., color, 1988, Front Range Education Media Corp., 1987 March On Washington is detailed.

ACityTV, Toronto, Canada

Growing Up Gay, approx 1 hr., color, 1985, Executive Producer: Mose Znaimer with Director: Randy Gulliver, Excellent at showing what it means to be a gay youth in Canada.

KQED - TV, San Francisco, California, Frontline Presents

Children of the Night, Director Paul Hinchel accurately depicts the San Francisco street life of a young gay man.

Individual Episodes

Quantum Leap - gay military cadet
20/20 - gay/lesbian youth suicide, gays in the military
Gabriel's Fire - outing
321 Contact - Ryan White's Story
Degrassi Junior High - older brother who's gay
Channel 9 News - Gay in the 90's
One Life to Live - gay teenage (continuing character)
Roseanne - gay employer (continuing character)
Law and Order - outing, murder of gay male
L.A. Law - lesbian lawyer (continuing character)
21 Jumpstreet - gay teenager living with AIDS
Doctor, Doctor - gay brother (continuing character)
Northern Exposure - city founders were lesbians
PrimeTime Live - born or bred
Dear John - a woman realizes she is a lesbian

192

PAMPHLETS/POSTERS
Pamphlets

Parents and Friends of Lesbians and Gays, P.O. Box 27605, Central Station, Washington, D.C. 20038.

About Our Children
Coming Out to Your Parents *
Why is My Child Gay
Respect All Youth Issue Papers by Ann Thompson Cook. *
   Who Is Killing Whom?
   You Can Help
   Youth and Homosexuality

Parent and Friends of Lesbians and Gays - Denver, P.O. Box 18901, Denver, CO 80218, (303) 333-0286.

Guidelines for Counselors
Plus the Lit. distributed by the National Assoc. listed above.

The Campaign to End Homophobia, P.O. Box 819, Cambridge, MA 02139, $10 with permission to reprint.

I think I Might Be Gay .. Now what do I do?
I think I Might be Lesbian .. Now what do I do?
Homophobia (What Causes It)
The Connections Between Homophobia and the Other "isms."

Illinois Gay and Lesbian Task Force, Youth and Education Committee, Attn. Al Wardell, 615 W. Wellington, Chicago, Illinois 60657.

I think I Might Be Gay .. Now what do I do? (a different version) *
I think I Might be Lesbian .. Now what do I do? (a different version) *

Fund for Human Dignity/National Gay and Lesbian Task Force, 666 Broadway, Room 410, NY, NY 10012, (212) 529-1600.

Coming Out (Spanish and English)
20 Questions about Homosexuality
Who's Behind the Gay Rights Movement
Answers to Parents Questions about Homosexuality
Combattling Homophobia
Workshops on Homophobia

Lesbian and Gay Public Awareness Project, P.O. Box 65603, LA, CA, 90065, (213) 281-1946.

Homophobia - what are we so afraid of?
In Our Own Image (positive portraits of lesbian and gays)

Hetrick-Martin Institute Inc., New York: Hetrick-Martin Institute, Inc. 401 West Street, New York, NY 10014, (212) 633-8920.

Tales of the Closet, Vol. 1-7 - Comic books depicting a diverse group of gay and lesbian teens in a Bronx High School. Each volumes deals with a different aspect like isolation, family, violence, health, pregnancy, and religion. Subject matter is not always dealt with in a positive light.

Posters

Hetrick-Martin Institue, Inc., 401 West Street, New York, New York 10014, (212) 633-8920.

You Are Not Alone (2 versions).

Illustration and Design by Martha Leonard, 1071 S. Clinton Ave., Rochester, New York 14620, 271-1467.

Celebrate - Our Differences

Illinois Gay and Lesbian Task Force, 615 West Wellington, Chicago, Illinois 60657-5305, (312) 975-0707.

If you, or someone you love is Gay or Lesiban - the school counselor has information that can help.

Tattered Cover Bookstore, 2955 East 1st Ave, Denver, CO 80206, (303) 322-7727.

Unfortunately, history has set the record a little too straight. (National Coming Out Day Poster - 1988).

Wingspan Ministry, St. Paul-Reformation Church, 100 North Oxford St., Saint Paul, MN 55104, (612) 224-3371.

This Attraction is in Your Neighborhood - Its About Love
What can you do if your best friend just told you 'I'm Gay'."

---

* Highly Recommended
** $250 Middle/Junior High School Library
*** $250 High School Library

Tracy Phariss, P.O. Box 280346, Lakewood, CO 80228-0346

194

NEVER AGAIN, NEVER FORGET: Lesbians and Gays In the Congressional Cemetery

The Congressional Cemetery, located near the Anacostia River, was established by the Washington Parish (Episcopal) in 1807 for all denominations of people who are recognized for their outstanding service to the federal government and the people of the USA. They are people who made our history representing areas of legislature, executive, armed forces, arts and sciences, healing arts, diplomacy and journalism.

PHOTO CAPTIONS

Plans to erect a mausoleum for Harvey Milk, the first openly gay person elected to public office in the USA - assassinated in San Francisco, 1978.

Visitors pay respects to the late Audre Lorde, lesbian-feminist, poet, writer who died of cancer, 1992. (top photo next page)

Flowers and blossoms adorn the burial site for Sgt. Leonard Matlovich, a gay Vietnam Veteran and the first American to challenge the ban on lesbians and gays in the military. Died of AIDS several years ago. Pink triangles frame his epitaph: "When I was in the military, they gave me a medal for killing two men and a discharge for loving one." (photo next page)

Photos by Paul Hennefeld

196

THE '93 MARCH ON WASHINGTON

Over a million march in the 1993 LESBIAN, GAY AND BISEXUAL MARCH ON WASHINGTON to demand equal rights for lesbians and gays, greater AIDS and breast/cervical cancer research, and lifting the ban on lesbians and gays in the military.

MARCH ON WASHINGTON **photos by Paul Hennefeld**

199

201

WE ARE EVERYWHERE   **photo by Terry Suruda**

The NAMES Project AIDS Memorial Quilt

Information and photos permission of Ben Carlson, Media Coordinator of the NAMES Project AIDS Memorial Quilt, 310 Townsend Street, San Francisco, Ca 94107.

In June of 1987, a small group of strangers gathered in a San Francisco storefront to document the lives they feared history would neglect. Their goal was to create a memorial for those who had died of AIDS, and to thereby help people understand the devastating impact of the disease...The Quilt was conceived in 1985 by long-time San Francisco gay rights activist Cleve Jones. Since the 1978 assassination of gay San Francisco Supervisor Harvey Milk, Jones had helped to organize the annual candlelight march honoring Milk. As he was planning, he learned that the number of San Franciscans lost to AIDS had passed the 1,000 mark. He was moved to ask each of the marchers to write on placards the names of friends and loved ones who had died of AIDS. At the end of the march, Jones and others stood on ladders, above the sea of candlelights, taping these placards to the walls of the Federal Building. To Jones, the wall of names looked like a patchwork quilt.

Today, the NAMES Project AIDS Memorial Quilt is a powerful visual reminder of the AIDS pandemic. More than 23,000 individual three-by-six foot memorial panel-each one remembering the life of someone who has died of complications related to AIDS -have been sewn together, coordinated for worldwide display.

Public response to the Quilt was immediate. People in each of the U.S. cities most affected by AIDS sent panels. Generous donors rapidly filled "wish lists" for sewing machines, office supplies and volunteers. Lesbians, gay men and their friends were especially supportive. As awareness of the Quilt grew, so did participation.

Photos by Matt Herron (top) and Marc Geller

The Quilt was nomination for a
Nobel Peace Prize in 1989 and again
in 1990. **COMMON THREADS:
STORIES FROM THE QUILT won the**
Academy Award as the best feature-
length documentary film of 1989.

"Yesterday I saw the
Quilt for the first time...
I was only going to take
a quick look and leave
...but instead...my life,
opinions and ideals
have been changed
forever."
                -A Quilt Visitor

Photos by Matt Herron(top);

Rick Reinhard and Debra L. Rottenberg.

APPENDIX

FROM 'PROJECT 10'

GAY AND LESBIAN ADOLESCENTS AND THEIR FAMILIES

Photo: Valerie Snyder   (L to R: Lamonta Pierson, Lynn Shepodd, Honey Ward)

"I'm proud of my lesbian daughter"

"It's been more than a decade since we at home were responding to Lynn's 'I'm gay' letter mailed from college. Reading it to the family, I suddenly knew I'd had a plan for Lynn, and this was off course.

She had had to put miles between us before making here announcement and I was feeling here courage. How terrible for her to have worried: 'Will they love me after they know . . . love me with restrictions . . . check me off?'

The process of my adjustment wasn't instant or without fluctuation, but I asked myself, what of real importance had changed? Lynn was still my pretty and winsome daughter, still the young woman, a crusader, bent on correcting every social and political shortcoming. Surely, she was entitled to here own life.

Twelve busy years have passed. My 'Lynn' file bulges with her writings, causes, and activities. It seems that her calling has always been political so that is where she works. She has established, with a perfect companion, a remarkable, loving home full of trust and respect.

Yes, I not only love my daughter, I am filled with a sense of pride and completion as her life unfolds."

Lamonta Pierson

© 1989 Lesbian and Gay Public Awareness Project

206

COMING OUT TO PARENTS, an excellent booklet for both parents and children is available without charge from Parents and Friends of Lesbians and Gays, Inc. P.O. Box 24565, Los Angeles, CA 90024. (Send SASE)

Among other things, this booklet discusses questions a person needs to consider before "coming out."

1. Are you sure about your sexual orientation?

2. Are you comfortable with your gay/lesbian sexuality?

3. Do you have support?

4. Are you knowledgeable about homosexuality?

5. What is the emotional climate at home?

6. Can you be patient?

7. What is your motive for coming out now?

8. Do you have available resources?

9. Are you financially dependent on your parents?

10. What is your general relationship with your parents?

11. What is their moral societal view?

12. Is this your decision?

Individual Conferencing

Individual conferencing can take place in many different ways. A student may have mentioned a critical incident in a class discussion or in a writing assignment, and the teacher wishes to inquire further. A student may ask to speak privately to a teacher. Perhaps a student's performance or behavior may have alerted the teacher to a possible incident. Or, a student may have been referred to a counselor or may have self-referred to some support person on the staff.

The following strategies have proven helpful in dealing with individual conferences with students in distress:

FIND PRIVACY--If possible, try to find a place where the student can be assured of some privacy. Perhaps a cubicle in the counselor's office or in some other office. Avoid placing yourself in a compromising situation. Don't go off campus. Stay visible to others.

ASSURE CONFIDENTIALITY--Within the legal limits, assure the student that what is said will remain confidential.

MAINTAIN CALM--It is very important that the adult present a balanced demeanor so that the student knows that he or she has permission to talk freely about the source of the distress.

BE HONEST WITH YOURSELF--Keep in touch with your own feelings and reactions to the student, the issues, and the situation. This is especially important in an emotionally laden subject like homosexuality. If you feel you cannot handle the situation, ask someone else to take over, and arrange the transition.

VALIDATE FEELINGS--Listen well to the feelings that are being expressed by the student. Help the student clarify feelings. Use gentle probes for clarification and elaboration. Use increasingly focused questions when appropriate.

PROVIDE INFORMATION--The correct information at the right time can be very helpful. Be sure not to preach, however, and be sure that your own need to "do something" is not clouding your judgement regarding the timeliness of the information.

EXPLORE RESOURCES--As soon as possible, explore with the student what resources he or she has available, and what their support system provides. Assist them in deciding who, when and how to reach out for that support.

IT IS NOT O.K.

This list was developed in one of Dr. Uribe's workshops during the summer of 1989. The 85 teachers and counselors present broke into groups and through comparison and elimination of redundant phrases, came up with this list, called THE NOT O.K. LIST.

IT IS NOT O.K. TO:

1. Name call or allow name calling in any language.

    It is totally unacceptable on the part of the adults, and should be monitored carefully when it happens among the students.

2. To say queer, fairy, Fairyfax, dyke, fag, faggot, butch, queen, sissy, maricon, culero or any other pejorative term.

3. To joke about one's sexual orientation or to tell jokes about homosexuals or to make AIDS jokes, etc.

4. It is not o.k. to say:
    How do you know?
    Are you sure? (when a student reveals sexual orientation)
    You will get over it when the right man/woman comes along.
    I don't agree with it, but I still like you.
    Have you tried dating the opposite sex?
    You will grow out of it.
    Do you think God is punishing you?
    Some of my best friends are.
    It's only a phase.
    Have you tried to change?
    I accept you but I don't agree with your choice.
    You are not normal.
    You don't look like one.
    You are sick.
    How did that happen?
    Don't you want to have children?
    You do have a problem.
    I don't want to hear about it.

What is wrong with you?
You are going to get AIDS.
I don't dislike homosexuals, it's what they do that I dislike.
Your family will reject you.
You won't be able to have a happy life.
Why don't you try to act more masculine/feminine?
You will embarrass the family.
Your parents won't love you.
What will your parents do?
You need counseling.

5. To talk about homosexuality as if it were a sickness or a deviance,
   or to say that gays caused AIDS, or that AIDS is a gay disease, or a
   punishment from God, or that PWA's should be isolated.

6. If a parent, do not say, where did I go wrong, or why are you doing
   this to me?

THE KINSEY CONTINUUM

Exclusively heterosexual behavior

Primarily heterosexual, but incidents of homosexual behavior

Primarily heterosexual, but more than incidental homosexual behavior

Equal amounts of heterosexual and homosexual behavior

Primarily homosexual, but more than incidental heterosexual behavior

Primarily homosexual, but incidents of heterosexual behavior

Exclusively homosexual behavior

Entering Adulthood: Living in Relationships

THE HARD REALITY OF LATINA LESBIANS (from Project 10, National Times - NOW)...In Latin America, to be a lesbian is intolerable. Family and society, influenced by the teachings of the church, look upon lesbians as social outcasts-without rights and privileges, unworthy of respect and the love of society, family and friends. Some lesbians have to choose exile as a way of surviving and exercising their (orientation).

Carmen left Ecuador ten years ago because she couldn't live in her country as a lesbian. Amelia, caught holding hands with her lover by her parents, was forced to leave Columbia virtually overnight because she had brought "shame" to her family. Maria Elena had to choose between emigrating to the US or facing jail in Cuba, even though she had taken an active part in the Cuban revolution...Even in the US though, Latina lesbians are confronted with multiple discrimination-as women, as Latinas, as immigrants, and as lesbians...Exile almost always brings economic disadvantages. Latinas in the US earn only 80 percent of a white woman's wages. Immigrants enter the work force in lover-paying jobs because they enter a job market that is new to them...Health care problems arise when health insurance is not available or not affordable...Added to (these) issues is the rejection Latina lesbians face from the Latino communities in the US where they settle, hoping to find a support network and cultural affinity once they are in this country...Latina lesbians spend every day of their lives facing the fact that they must be invisible in order to survive. They hide from their own Latino communities, from the Anglo-American society that looks down on them, and from themselves.

Latina lesbians must be included in the movement to bring about equality for all women, with the recognition that issues are often different from white lesbians. Inclusion can empower.

STORY OF CHRIS (Origin of Project 10)...It all began in November, with an incident (which involved) an openly gay male who had been transferred to Fairfax from another school. From the day he entered, he was physically abused by peers, and verbally abused by teachers and peers alike. Finally, he dropped out of school entirely and turned to the streets, becoming one more casualty of a system that neither understood nor cared about him. He rejection was a systematic repeat of his experiences at four other schools. This offensive incident prompted an investigation into the school history and background of Chris H., age 17, African-American, male homosexual. Two counselors, seven former teachers and the head of a group home where he lived were located. Chris had been forcibly ejected from his home at age 14 for admitting he was gay and had been on the streets for a year until he was placed in a juvenile home and finally a residential home for gay and lesbian youth. All his former teachers and counselors described him as "sweet," "nice," and of average intelligence with no particular learning disabilities. The only reason given as to why he

encountered so much trouble in school was that he was gay. The story was always the same. He would enter a school, and the students would begin harassing him immediately. If he defended himself, either verbally or physically, he was taken to the dean's office and reprimanded. Chris had been submitted to so much abuse at one school that there was a letter in his file, from an administrator at the Gay and Lesbian Community Services Center, registering a protest. The response, to transfer him out.

212

LEAVING CONFUSION BEHIND
by Gail Watnick

Why did she do this to me? First of all, she did not tell me first. She told everyone else and not me. I heard from the "everyone else" group that she is moving. Wow, she really is moving. How utterly insane.

673-8845

"Hello, why didn't you tell me you were moving? I heard it from someone else. You know of course you cannot move. I mean, remember how we planned out the rest of our years together until college. you know we were going to continue being clueless together in French class until we became seniors. Who am I going to kid around with in French class now? Hold on just a minute. You told me you were going to find me some awesome guy, and we were going to go out on a double date. What about that? When is that going to happen now that you are moving? I can not believe you are going away. Are you just pulling my leg? I really don't want to believe it. School is going to be so boring without you."

I wondered if she knew how I was feeling at that moment. I wondered if she felt the same. The feeling of loss and loneliness overwhelmed me.

"You are my best friend, and you are leaving me. I just can't see how you could do this. You don't even seem to care."

"Gail, it's not my decision, and I'm not happy to be leaving."

"Well, then why don't you just stay here?"

"What? You're being crazy."

"I know. It's just that I'm going to miss you tons."

213

Our last time together was truly an enlightening experience for me. We were at a pool party at the end of the school year. I was really enjoying myself. It was the last time I would see all of my friends before I went to the Cape for the summer. We were dancing, playing goofy games, and talking about the past and the coming summer. I then decided to go swimming. A combination of water games and splashing added to the excitement. I joined with enthusaism.

After a bit, people slowly began vacating the pool until I was the only one left. The water felt wonderfully cool against my body. It was an enormous relief to be able to stand in the water and forget about school and the fact that she was leaving. Thoughts of the summer crept into my head: *I pictured myself walking along the street in the tiny Cape village. My eyes inspect everyone in the crowd of people who walks by me. Every now and then the inspection becomes a deep probing. Occasionally one of those probed people casually brushes against my shoulder as she passes. Into the art gallery I stroll and attempt to follow the sculptures and pictures that line the walls. However, the people are much more interesting sights, and I am drawn out onto the street into the crowds. My eyes pass over the neon signs, the new wave sparkling shops, and the nifty clothing shops which attempt to lure the passerby shopper. Since I'm not your typical shopper, however, none of these shops interest me. Yet earlier, as I headed toward the street, my intention was to shop like a typical shopper. Something is odd. What am I shopping for? My mind is not processing the answer to that question. I seem a bit confused. Sitting on a bench, I attempt to sublimate my confusion and focus on the crowds. Scrutinizing begins again. As the night progresses, the families and little children gradually leave the street, and couples begin to make their grand*

214

entrance. My eyes avidly watch (studying the tableau put in front of me), relaying the message to my body which in turn does its own exploration. I am mesmerized by the sight of the people holding onto one another. Suddenly my eyes are caught by a peculiar looking couple - a woman and a man. I am surprised to see it is she, and wonder who she is with. Near realization. As I rise from the bench, confusion rises too and I leave the street.

I am still alone in the pool, casually dipping my hand into the water to make rippling circular patterns, my reflection in the outermost ring of circles.

"Hey, Gail, come on out of the pool. The food is hot right now, but it won't be for long."

My pondering has made me extremely quiet and pensive. I get out of the pool, change my clothes, and join the others. Once again I see her. I am confused again. In my mind, she was just on the street holding onto that man. Where is the man? It does not matter. she is moving. When will I see her again? I eat in silence. I am not thinking. My mind is too confused. I am just breathing, and I am surrounded by people who I do not understand.

I feel a tap on my shoulder. She stands in front of me and asks me to come outside with her. I go out and listen to her as she begins to speak.

"Gail, why have you suddenly become so solemn?"

I think about her question, feeling her strong presence, yet her words become inaudible. Tears slowly fill my eyes, and then begin to flow freely. Quietly, the words slip out, "I don't want you to go." She puts her arms around me and comforts me until the tears subside.

Her hug made me feel it. It was then that I realized why I would miss her so much.

She moved away and so did my confusion.

215

Additional Curricula - Respect for Diversity; Building Bridges
prepared by Sue McConnell-Celi

~ *STUDENT PLAYWRIGHTS: Students play-act a female/male skit of a recent popular TV show with one exception - two females or two males are substituted. Discuss audience reaction to dialogue and body gestures. Various racial, ethnic, socioeconomic, age, dis/abled groups may be used. Focus on 'self-empowerment' as alternate to 'power-over'.*

~ *RESEARCH PROJECTS: (1) Trace AIDS from its first appearance over two decades ago. Compare with present findings; draw conclusions. What programs can the school initiate in educating youth about AIDS? (2) Examine the progression of Lesbian and Gay coverage in the media since the Stonewall Riot, 1969. Pay particular attention to the text and language used by the film world, pop culture in magazines or newspaper coverage. (Maria Perez, entertainer, contributed idea #2 by sending a thesis she completed while in college; she has also co-authored an article, published in Network on the topic, Women and AIDS). Research project goals: Students will obtain information/reinforce library skills.*

~ *USING THE NEWSPAPER: (1) During class, hold a mock press conference with two students who pretend to be a lesbian or gay celebrity. Reporters carefully prepare questions beforehand, take accurate notes, and write an article on the superstars. (2) Write a "Dear Abby" letter from the standpoint of a lesbian or gay student, dis/abled, homeless, or person of color. Another student will respond to each letter with positive, meaningful advice. (3) Teacher selects current events covering diversity; s/he separates each story from its headline. Students then match the headlines with the appropriate stories. (Can also make a sequence skill of this by cutting out paragraphs and tossing them in a box).*

~ *The term "civil rights" is frequently discussed. What does it mean for a student to have these rights? What steps can students themselves take to achieve/maintain human rights in school? Classmates list specific ways in which they can insure that students are happy and treated with respect. Target actions that contribute to physical safety and consideration of others' feelings, as well as those that inhibit learning and communication. Make posters.*

216

CREATING A QUILT PANEL (Can be a classroom project).

The memorial panels that make up the NAMES Project AIDS Memorial Quilt were made by all sorts of people, in all kinds of colors, fabrics, and styles. You do not have to be a professional artist or a sewing expert to create a moving personal tribute. It doesn't matter if you use paint or fine needle work; any remembrance is appropriate. You may choose to create a panel privately, as a personal memorial to someone you've loved, but we encourage you to follow the traditions of old-fashioned sewing and quilting bees, and include friends, family, and co-workers. Just follow these steps:

1. Design the panel: Include the name of the one you are remembering; feel free to include additional information such as dates of birth and death, and hometown. Limit each panel to one individual...Write a two-page letter about the person and yourself.
2. Choose your materials: Remember that the Quilt is folded and unfolded many times so durability is crucial. A medium-weight, non-stretch fabric such as a cotton duck or poplin works best. The finished panel must be 3 feet by 6 feet (90cm x 180cm), so when you cut the fabric leave an extra 2-3 inches on each side for a hem. If you can't do it yourself, NAMES people will do it.
3. Can us these techniques: Applique, paint (colorfast dye), stencil (use textile paint), collage (avoid glass and sequins) and photos.
4. If you can, make a financial contribution to help pay for the cost of adding your panel to the Quilt. (Gifts of over $250 will be acknowledged in the Annual Report).

Photo by Marc Geller
NAMES Quilt photos courtesy of NAMES Project AIDS Memorial Quilt

This letter was found posted on the refrigerator door -

Dear Mom,
        I'm a homosexual.
I'll be home around
10 tonight.
                Love,
                Keith